A Reason For Hope

A REASON FOR HOPE

LIBERATION THEOLOGY CONFRONTS A LIBERAL FAITH

by Fredric John Muir

SUNFLOWER INK
37931 Palo Colorado Road, Carmel, California 93923

ACKNOWLEDGEMENTS

Permission to publish material from the following sources is hereby greatfully acknowledged:

Lawrence Swain, for "The Case for a Unitarian Universalist Left", 1989, an unpublished manuscript.

David O. Rankin, for "Thoughts Following a Suicide" in *Portraits from the Cross*, UUA, 1978.

Library of Congress Catalogue Number 93-086732
ISBN 0-931104-39-4

iv

Table Of Contents

Preface

At the 1989 General Assembly of the Unitarian Universalist Association, William R. Jones spoke on the topic "Theology and Activism." Noting the importance that Unitarian Universalists give the principle of equality as well as the role of equality in liberation theology, Jones stated that for Unitarian Universalists to develop a liberation theology, they would have to relinquish some of their socioeconomic power. Only in this way could the balance of power needed for equality be achieved. Judith Meyer, in responding to Jones's talk, asked Jones if he felt a "theology of relinquishment" might be developed among religious liberals. He was not hopeful, though not hopeless, about this possibility: the risks would be high, it would be very threatening.

Jones is one of the Association's most creative, energetic, and outspoken leaders. I took his critique as a challenge. "What is the alternative?" I can remember asking myself. Failure to develop a theology that would set us on the path away from oppression and toward liberation is not only critical to the well-being of Unitarian Universalism, but in terms of personal theo-ethical values it is imperative. It will mean change, a different way of viewing ourselves in church and in community.

During the years that this book has been written (and since Jones's lecture), events have shaken and shaped the world unlike anything in decades - often beyond our dreams: the redesigning of Eastern Europe and the Soviet Union; destruction of the earth's rain forests; the freeing of Nelson Mandela and reform in South Africa; the destruction of the Berlin Wall; global warming; war in the Persian Gulf; Latin American peoples continuing to fight for a life free of oppression. Changes occur so quickly that it has become difficult to keep up! A similar kind of essence-shaking (and shaping) is going to be necessary for Unitarian Universalism if it is to alter its ways and move toward the kind of empowerment and equality encouraged by liberation theology. Examining the core of our religious tradition and faith is critical if we are to be hopeful, and not hopeless, about our future. I am hopeful. This work is one way of sharing that hope.

The hope that has nurtured and supported the effort to produce this work has strong roots. It has come from three sources: The Rev. Don Wheat of the Third Unitarian Church and his wife Anne, and my parents John and Charlene Muir, who early on taught me the difference hope can make; the people of the Unitarian Universalist Church of Annapolis, Maryland, who shared with me not only their hope but their time; and most of all my family, my wife, Karen, and my children, Kristina and Andrew, who have shared their dreams with me, and whose patience and endurance during these years have given me hope beyond my wildest dreams.

A REASON FOR HOPE

LIBERATION THEOLOGY CONFRONTS A LIBERAL FAITH

Chapter One

INTRODUCING LATIN AMERICAN LIBERATION THEOLOGY

INTRODUCING LATIN AMERICAN LIBERATION THEOLOGY

Liberation theology is not a theological movement,
but a theology in movement.

Leonardo & Clodovis Boff

On a visit home during my first year of seminary, my pastor invited me to his house for coffee and conversation. It wasn't long after arriving that he wanted to know, "So, what is the newest theology everyone is studying?" His excited anticipation was deflated when I told him "liberation theology." "That's it, liberation theology? That's ridiculous, all theology is liberation theology. I don't get it." Now, thinking back to his response, I'm reminded of a conversation I heard about between a theologian from the North Atlantic community and one from Latin America. The Latino asked the Northerner: "Why do you insist on calling our theology *liberation* theology. For us, *it is theology*." The fact of the matter is that all theologies are not the same: not all theology is about liberation and certainly not all people see themselves in need of liberation. Liberation theology exists (as do all theologies, that is, interpretations of faith experience) because not everyone is confronted with the same life experiences and histories. Kathleen Talvacchia writes:

> Liberation theologians have taught us that a person's location within a society's power structure affects how that person interprets what is real and what is true. In the U.S., theology done from the perspective of those who have traditionally lacked power and suffered social oppression - the poor, African Americans, women, homosexuals, Native Americans, and Asians - not only changes the way we do theology, but creates a new set of

~~criteria~~ for theological truth. *(Talvacchia, 232)*

All theology has an origin - the person performing the interpretive task. The task, the work of theology, is always completed from a particular interpretive stance. This is what Dietrich Bonhoeffer was doing when he wrote:

> There remains an experience of incomparable value. We have for once learnt to see the great events of world history from below, from the perspective of the outcast, the suspects, the maltreated, the powerless, the oppressed, the reviled - in short, from the perspective of those who suffer. *(Brown 1978, 50)*

This is not to suggest that Bonhoeffer was a liberation theologian. But he does present us with an unlikely interpretive stance - in the sense that we might not deliberately choose to see life circumstances "from below." And yet, this is the stance of Latin American Liberation Theology; it is theology that originates from "the underside of history," from the viewpoint of the poor.

Implicit in this "below-ness" are two points. Traditionally, theology begins in theory, in the classroom and then "trickles down" to the masses. I was told in seminary that congregations are always 10 to 20 years behind what is coming out of the academy. Latin American Liberation Theology begins with the masses, often in the absence of an academic education; "....all the themes of faith emerge from the streets rather than the library" (King 1988, 149). Second, it is in this sense that liberation theology is "organic" (King, 149). It begins with experience and not theory. It begins with the experience of the poor, of those from "below." As theology, this is the faith of the poor - a reflection on faith (Christian faith) in the eyes of the outcast.

Two unique themes arise from this place of origin. First, liberation theology is *contextual*; that is, it emerges out of and speaks to a specific set of circumstances and conditions. As *Latin American* Liberation Theology it speaks to Latin America. It doesn't claim to be a theology for all, but is specific to the context in which it was born. Every theology must speak to the situation of its proponents. Latin American Liberation Theology can be described "....in terms of three closely related tasks:"

> To interpret Christian faith in terms of the bleak lot of
> the poor; to criticize society and its ideologies through
> theology; and to observe and comment on the practices
> of the church itself... *(Berryman 1987, 8)*

The second theme is that Latin American Liberation Theology does not start in theory, but in movement or action, in *praxis*, which comes close to suggesting "practice," though this assocation is not exact. Praxis is the dynamic interrelationship between action and theory. In praxis, action and theory work only because of the other: each grows, supports and stays vibrant due to the other's viability. Praxis then, is more than practice - it is action informed by theory informed by action, etc. This process leads to a theological-breaking distinction:

> Because it is not merely cerebral but action-oriented as
> well, some are insisting that the Christian's task is not
> "ortho-doxy," e.g., right thinking, but "ortho-praxis," e.g.,
> the right combination of thinking and doing. *(Brown, 71)*

Inherent in the liberating nature of Latin American Liberation Theology is a critique of the status quo - the existing economic, religious, and social realities that keep the poor powerless. The question for liberation theology is how to integrate faith with politics. Those touched are not the dissatisfied, secularized man and woman, but the oppressed, those living with injustice (Boff 1989, 41).

Through a multi-tiered approach that combines context, praxis, theology, and the social sciences, the Boffs suggest that liberation theology is acted out on three levels (Boff 1987, 83). First, on a popular level, that is, the "ground" of the poor, the people themselves help to shape their society and future. The Boffs identify this as the level of "oral theology." Second is the pastoral level, focusing on the poor "so as to inspire the church to struggle for liberation." Finally, on the professional level, liberation theology enters the academy where it is subject to analysis, hermeneutics, and theoretical application. This tri-level paradigm is suggestive of the praxis framework by which action <--> theory works. Uniting the three levels in praxis "is the one basic assumption (that) faith transforms history, or, as others would put it, history seen from the basis of the ferment of faith" *(Boff 1987, 14).*

The Soul of Liberation Theology

Several concepts in liberation theology are critical to its formation. Basic to Latin American Liberation Theology is the experience of poverty, the condition under which those from below live. Poverty, then, is the reality from the underside of history; it is the reason for liberation. Gustavo Gutierrez writes: "....to be poor means to die of hunger, to be illiterate, to be exploited by others, not to know that you are being exploited, not to know that you are a person" (Gutierrez 1973, 289).

Inherent in Latin American Liberation Theology is a profound criticism of the world economy and related systems that result in the dehumanization of people. "Humanization" means not only the meeting of basic, specific life-sustaining economic needs, but in general, reversing the life-denying circumstances that produce "a situation in which a certain group of countries have their economies conditioned by the development and expansion of another country's economy" (McGovern 1989, 274).

Humanization, then, is freedom and yet more than freedom - humanization involves more than the freedom to choose and make decisions. Distinct from cultures, especially in the West, in which freedom and liberation are considered nearly synonymous, Latin American (and societies in which oppression is commonplace) liberation has a somewhat different characterization: "....it bears a relationship to 'life,' which, in its complexity, includes freedom, but is more basic" (Sobrino 1983, 66).

For those in poverty, the simple freedom of choice that we take for granted as primary is meaningless and purposeless without the more essential basics of humanization. This is to say, non-personhood as caused by poverty makes the act of choice a cruel hoax. Without a release from the oppression caused by poverty, humanization and then the possibility of exercising choice remains out of reach.

Understanding poverty as dehumanization, that is, as the denial of life-sustaining needs, is central to an understanding of liberation theology. It is clearly chief among the issues being addressed by Latin American theologians.[1] But two other understandings of poverty in the liberation paradigm are helpful to clarifying liberation theology in the Latin American context as well as our own. Both of these are of a different character, yet a form of poverty to be reckoned with.

One of these is what Unitarian Universalist theologian James Luther Adams refers to as "confidence" (Adams 1976, 13), or trust in something other than one's own ability to create an answer or alternative to dehumanization. This form of poverty is not directly related to socio-economics. Here poverty is an attitude toward life that is stripped not only of materialism but of other "essentials" taken for granted in daily living. Call it a poverty of spirit (that opens to God) or a self-denying acceptance of transforming power, it is the unguarded and faithful embracing of the "....inescapable, for no one can live without somehow coming to terms with it" (Adams, 13). Buechner speaks of this experience coming from a stance toward the world (in the world):

> [it is]...the same ecstatic and inexpressable experience which might be summarized as, at one and the same time, the total loss and total realization of self in merging with the ultimately Real. *(Buechner 1984, 60)*

In this experience of total loss and total realization, a person is completely open to the universe. In this experience of poverty, a person surrenders what is his or hers to the most elementary of conditions. But even in this condition of poverty, according to Adams, a new wealth of meaning is found and embraced:

> [The meaning]....is commanding, for it provides the structure or the process through which existence is main-

tained and by which any meaningful achievement is re-
alized. Indeed, every meaning in life is related to this
commanding meaning....*(Adams, 13)*

Another understanding of poverty results from solidarity with those from below, becoming "as" the poor in three
ways. One can support humanization in the most indirect
- yet critical - of ways via community-sponsored opportunities for giving, such as donations to the Salvation Army
and food banks or by fundraising for homeless shelters.
More direct service toward eliminating dehumanization
might include work at a shelter, volunteering in a soup
kitchen, or in some other way more directly assisting persons. Finally, there is living among the poor. While it is
impossible for a person of a Western, middle-class back-
ground to become as the dehumanized poor, the intimacy
achievable through the experience of living among the
poor can result in an effective solidarity.

The Boffs conclude:

> Whichever level is chosen, one point is paramount: any-
> one who wants to elaborate relevant liberation theo-logy
> must be prepared to go into the "examination hall" of the
> poor. Only after sitting on the benches of the humble
> will he or she be entitled to enter a school of "higher
> learning." *(Boff 1987, 24)*

Another important theme to Latin American Liberation
Theology is the preferential option for the poor. Simply
stated, this means that people professing a liberation out-
look keep uppermost in their minds "siding" with or working for the poor. Working for the poor can result in humanization. Showing a preferential option for the poor
means coming down on the side of the poor in work or
play, at home, with friends, in church. But in Latin American Liberation Theology, the concept of the preferential option means more: it is belief that *God* holds a preferential
option for the poor as well. For Unitarian Universalists,
this aspect of liberation theology is provoctive for two reasons.

First, it suggests that God, by virtue of this choosing, is

a being with deliberateness and consciousness. Many Unitarian Universalists would reject this characterization. Second, the idea that God categorically favors the poor - takes their "side" - implies there will be "winners" and "losers" in a kind of struggle for God's favor. This characterization is easily conceived by Unitarian Universalists as lacking in respect for the values of freedom, reason, and tolerance that are the Untiarian Universalist "trinity" of principles. Clearly, then, theological work must be done to make it possible for those of the liberal faith to contextualize the concpet of preferential option.

The input of Latin American theologians who have struggled with different concepts of God is important to this discussion. Croatto, for example, provides an excellent summary and contextualization of God's qualities in the liberation paradigm. He writes that there is a transcendent force that humans believe pervades everything of meaning in their world. People are in awe of this force and confess their powerlessness before it. In both its personified and non-personified forms, there are several aspects to it. The transcendent force is seen as life, as all-*knowledgeable*, and as the *origin* of everything. It brings *order* to what could be chaos. And, Croatto adds, "We could add a fifth ontological aspect: that of the sacred as *being*, but the expression of this aspect always revolves around the dynamic and operative [other] meanings" (Croatto 1983, 28).

While all these possibilities might be overwhelming, Adams suggests we need these options because "the word 'God' is so heavily laden with unacceptable connotations that it is for many people scarcely usable without confusion" (Adams, 13). Still, he insists that to have at least sensed that there is "that reality which works in nature, history, and thought and under certain conditions creates human good in human community" (Adams, 14).

The idea of God or "reality" imbued with such strong intention and deliberateness so as to "work in nature, history" and so forth is an idea that will face opposition among many Unitarian Universalists as well as and others of liberal faith. Members of the liberal faith seek a reality that is neutral not only because they object to the notion of an omnipotent force taking on human-like qualities (such as decision making), but also because they perceive that a God who plays favorites, cannot be impartial and all-loving. To side with one person or group is to not side with the other; it places one group against another. Such an action is neither reasonable nor tolerant - two principles that Unitarian Universalists hold dear.

If believers of liberal faith affirm an impartial, neutral God, it would follow that acting in ways inimical to this Neutrality would not be in their best interests. Those who affirm the ideals of neutrality, impartiality, and tolerance must respond to the liberationists' criticism that refusing to stake out a position - not choosing, that is - is in fact taking a position against the poor who did not end up on the underside as a result of anyone's neutrality! The poor are on the underside because of people and events which supported or refused to speak out and act against dehumanization.

To believe in a God of neutrality, in a God who does not choose sides, to believe in a God who does not show a preferential option for the poor, is to seek something other than humanization for the poor. To those who would stake out a claim of neutrality, Robert McAfee Brown writes:

> To think that we can be neutral in today's world is to believe that we can fail to be present, that we can afford the luxury of being simply absent, taking no sides, no options. We are all present one way or another in this historical moment and *we either contribute to the liberation of the oppressed of the world or we contribute to exploitation and injustice. (Brown 1978, 117)*

For some, the question of neutrality circles around the issue regarding the church's involvement in social justice. While Unitarian Unversalism has a heritage of prophetic vision, debate over the realities of "spirituality and liberation" (Brown 1988) continues as it does in many other middle-class churches: Is the role of the church to meet the individual spiritual needs of those in the congregation or to extend its concern and resources to those beyond its walls? Is there a relationship between spirituality and liberation?

The issue is not easily resolved, but it must be discussed openly and honestly, congregation by congregation. If nothing else, a Unitarian Universalist Theology of Liberation rests on the forthrightness with which Liberal Faith can address the causes and issues of poverty among our sisters and brothers worldwide.

It is only with this kind of candidness and open discussion of the issues that a contextual liberation theology will develop in the praxis of a local congregation. As in the oral tradition of popular and pastoral liberation theology, praxis will yield the kind of profundity that makes the Reign of God commonplace. This concept of the Reign of God is a final liberation theme I will address.

The Reign of God, derived from the biblical idea of the Kingdom of God, is a utopian concept, a dream, a hope that will remain out of the hands of the total worldwide community since, in part at least, the conditions that produce poverty and oppression are constant. These conditions are as basic to the human situation as are the assumptions that give rise to the Reign concept. Dorrien expands on this:

> The words are from Rauschenbush: "We shall never have a perfect life, yet we must seek it with faith. At best, there is always but an approximation to a just social order. The kingdom [Reign] of God is always but coming. But every approximation to it is worthwhile." That is the living spirit of a North American liberationism. *(Dorrien 1990, 274)*

South African liberation theologian John de Gruchy writes of the Reign in both a "social order" context and a pastoral one:

> ....I am convinced that the layperson, and by no means only the Christian believer, is hungry for genuine theological insight....But it must be stressed that this hunger will take different forms in different cultures, as well as in different social and political contexts. The hunger for meaning and the thirst for righteousness and social justice belong together. But whatever its form, such hunger and thirst is constant to the human condition. It is the

concern to make some sense out of life, suffering and death. *(de Gruchy 1986, 136-137)*

In this sense, the Reign of God could mean a period in time when people will be equal in the sense that their "hunger for meaning and their thirst for righteousness and social justice" will be satisfied.

There are then two sides to the Reign and together they form a dialectic that has been present and persistent throughout the history of humankind. On one side of this dialectic is "the concern to make some sense out of life, suffering and death," as suggested by de Gruchy. When faced with a life that is meaningless, especially when the meaninglessness is imposed from the outside, the response could be an urge to rebel, revolt, to respond in some way, even though, as in the case of political oppression, the consequences could be swift and severe. As de Gruchy notes, this hunger (and by implication the responses to it) will manifest itself differently in different cultures, but it will always be present, whether it appears through personal or political, spiritual or secular channels, or a combination of these.

Opposed to the oppression that produces meaninglessness is the constant need to exercise our "God-given" freedom to make choices and to decide and act even when it might appear that it is not in our best interest. Choice and decision making is basic to all human life, and to attempt to strip any person of these rights is to tamper with what makes for humanization.

Though not a part of the Unitarian Universalist vocabulary, the concept of the Reign of God can have meaning for religious liberals. An understanding of the Reign of God and its application can enrich Unitarian Universalism enabling us to make a commitment to the struggle for social justice as set forth by Gutierrez:

> The theology of liberation attempts to reflect on the experience and meaning of the faith based on the commitment to abolish injustice and to build a new society; this theology must be verified by the practice of that commitment, by active, effective participation in the struggle

which the exploited social classes have undertaken against their oppressors. Liberation from every form of exploitation, the possibility of a more human and more dignified life, the creation of a new man - all pass through this struggle. *(Gutierrez 1973, 307)*

Biblical Roots

Liberation theology is biblical, but not literalist or fundamentalist (Berryman 1986, 61). Reading through the eyes of the poor, scriptures raise and speak to issues of oppression, equality, empowerment, human interdependency, wealth, and justice. For Unitarian Universalists (and others of liberal religion), these issues are also important theo-ethical themes.

Unitarian Universalism's roots are in the Jewish and Christian traditions. Though it has moved away from the dogma and creeds of the traditional church (especially in the United States), the continuing influence of Christian and Jewish theology and reflection is critical to contemporary Unitarian Universalist thought and expression, which is reflected throughout the Unitarian Universalist Association's *Principles and Purposes.* Generally then, liberation theology and Unitarian Universalism share a common point of departure as well as a continuing expression of faith stemming from biblical liberation themes. Specifically, there are at least five themes, which taken together, compose a shared heritage and starting point.

First, creation is good (Genesis 1 - 2:4a & 1:4b - 25). According to the creation story, humanity did not begin as unequal partners in sin, but as equals in good. Each person is unique and special; no person has an innate authority over another. According to the creation story, people were created in the image of God, and so all human life is equal and sacred. These themes from the creation account take contemporary expression for Unitarian Universalists in the first two principles of the Association's *Principles and Purposes:*

> We covenant to affirm and promote:
> The inherent worth and dignity of every person
> Justice, equity and compassion in human relations
> *(Principles and Purposes , 1984)*

Second, we have a covenant with creation. With all of creation's living and non-living parts, we form a covenanted unity. "Covenant " has historically meant an agreement that is binding; a covenant is not something to be entered into lightly. The covenant of the creation story, a covenant between God and humans, is an implied one. Humans are not at the center of creation, but are a part of it. But having been created in God's image, humans' status and authority are unrivaled. This uniqueness is identity-forming in that it creates a relationship and a context out of which identity can grow (Adams 1991, 241). It also can be illusory, leading to the belief of mastery and domination (Granberg-Michaelson 1990, 28-29). Unitarian Universalism gives expression to this covenant and these concerns in this way:

> We covenant to affirm and promote:
> Acceptance of one another....
> Respect for the interdependent web of all existence
> of which we are a part. *(Principles and Purposes 1984)*

Third, justice is good and humans must take sides, as God does, with those who suffer from injustice (this is the preferrential option). Taking the side of justice is the message of the Exodus Story (Ex. 3:7-10) as well as the message of the prophets (e.g., Micah 6:8). Siding with the poor and working for justice means bringing about the Kingdom of God today: "....the Kingdom of God necessarily implies the reestablishment of justice in this world..." (Gutierrez 1973, 298).

For religious liberals, the phrase "The Kingdom of God" might be an awkward one. Richard Gilbert suggests that the phrase "The Beloved Community" is in keeping with both the biblical tradition as well as the liberal religious one (Gilbert, 101). The Beloved Community is the principle that Unitarian Universalists covenant to affirm and promote: "The goal of world community with peace, liberty and justice for all" *(Principles and Purposes, 1984)*.

A fourth theme is the message of prophecy. The denunciation of idolatry and injustice by the Old Testament prophets is clear (e.g., Amos 5:21-24; Isaiah 3:14-15). The prophetic role was not to provide social services, but to be a critic and advocate for the poor (Gilbert 117):

> We see the prophet as one who stands at the edge of a community's experience and tradition, under the Great Taskmaster's eye, viewing human life from a piercing perspective and bringing an imperative sense of the perennial and inescapable struggle of good against evil, of justice again injustice. In the name of the Holy One the prophet shakes us out of our pride and calls for a change of heart and mind and action. With fear and trembling the prophet announces crisis and demands ethical decision here and now. (*Adams 1986, 99*)

James Adams promotes the liberal religious idea of "the prophethood of all believers" (Adams, 102). Working together in this prophethood, Unitarian Universalists covenant to affirm and promote:

> A free and responsible search for truth and meaning. The right of conscience and the use of the democratic process.....

The fifth theme shared by both the biblical and Unitarian Universalist traditions is summarized in Jesus' stated mission and ministry in Luke 4:18:

> The Spirit of the Lord is upon me, because he has annointed me to bring good news to the poor. He has sent me to proclaim release to the captives and recovery of sight to the blind, to let the oppressed go free....

This was a ministry to people in *this* world, for those who are living without justice, under oppression. Jesus' ministry was one of serving not only those in spiritual poverty, but physical and material poverty. It was this same ideal that William Ellery Channing spoke about, a tradition and model idealized by religious liberals for over a century:

> Religion, we are told, is a private, personal thing, a con-

15

cern between the individual and God. His neighbor or the community must not meddle with it....I would maintain that religion is eminently *a social principle*, entering into social life, having most important bearings on the public weal....The social character of religion is not sufficiently regarded. *(Gilbert 1980, 22)*

"Concientizacion"

Having heard the basic thrust of Latin American Liberation Theology as well as having started a process by which central themes can be identified, explored, and contextualized, it is now important to work toward conscientization or critical consciousness-raising (Fiorenza 1989, 318). Through this important step, we can listen to the message of Latin American Liberation Theology on its own terms, hear its claims against the North Atlantic, Euro-centric community, and begin reflection and commitment toward reshaping our message of liberation (Brown 1989, 494).

Segundo Galilea looks at the process of conscientization as one of evangelizing: "The poor evangelize us because service to them widens our experience to God, makes us more contemplative...." (Galilea 1988, 139). This is a process of attitude formation, of attitude-changing. It occurs when, directly or indirectly, one sides with the poor. One attitude that is crucial to change is ethnocentrism.

Due to the environment in which we have been raised and educated, we are culture-bound. We see the world with a limited view - we cannot help but do so. Showing a preferential option for the poor widens our perspective and helps to remove the blindness caused by ethnocentrism. This is one way that we come to hear the poor. From the challenge of Latin American Liberation Theology, "...the condition of the poor and suffering of our society inspires and points out the concrete options that we must make in our lifestyle..." (Galilea, 27)

Second, the poor offer us the opportunity to achieve wholeness or balance, to make congruent the interior life with the exterior life. Call it being or doing, spirituality or liberation, contemplation or commitment, trying to hold these two in balance is difficult. To tell the history of this tension is to tell the story of the church. Conscientization can lead to a fuller understanding of and appreciation for the spiritual and liberating dynamics of any person. When the tension between contemplation and commitment is not high - is without the kind of tautness that reflective consciousness-raising can promote - one is thrown off mentally, emotionally, and physically.

Finally, through critical consciousness-raising, awareness of the message from below can break through our ethnocentrism and in this there is the hope that paternalism will no longer be the mindset from which we do outreach. Collaboration and not paternalism is the spirit in which time is spent with the poor and community is created. This means an attitude of being at one with the poor, in solidarity with them, and not being as a separate person coming in from the outside (a better side) to "help" or "save." Paternalistic attitudes only reinforce the ethnocentrism that keeps our blindness in place and prohibits changes in our views, and values. Paternalism discourages humanization.

"Conscientizacion" is an important step for those of us in the North Atlantic community; "conscientizacion" begins a process of turning away from longheld assumptions and characterizations of the poor, and of opening up to the conversion brought about by a transformation opportunity. Berryman writes about this transformation:

> Those whose radicalization process has been nonreligious can nevertheless find familiar landmarks in what I have just described: experience with the poor, the violence used by power structures, the growing awareness of systemic connections. Those Christians I have in mind, however, also see this process as a "conversion." The word may conjure up a dramatic emotional event - St. Paul struck on the way to Damascus, or revival participants "repenting and declaring for Jesus" - but the biblical word refers to a basic shift in mindset, attitude, and life orientation. This is what the experience I have been outlining is all about. *(Berryman 1986, 156)*

Still, it will not be possible to completely shed cultural context regardless of how deep one's commitment to the poor. We must not seek to lose our culture, but to learn about the poor, to learn *from* the poor, and then in turn to speak to our context - to work in collaboration with the poor. The importance of context is what Gustavo Gutierrez refers to when he writes that the "songs" of religious people may be one song only of different lands:

> ....But the songs are sung by persons in particular histori-
> cal situations, and these provide the framework within
> which they perceive God's presence and
> also God's absence. (Gutierrez 1984, 7)

A New Myth

We reach an understanding of Latin American Liberation Theology through contextualization, an understanding of common Biblical themes, consciousness raising, and praxis. In other words, we move closer to the poor as our perception of the underside of history grows clearer. In this theology of movement, we come to understand ourselves better. Marc Ellis notes: "As in any movement outward toward those who are suffering, it is at the same moment a movement toward the deepest themes of [one's] community life...." (Ellis 1989, 386)

As Brown suggests, a liberation theology for those outside the Latin American experience must be contextualized (Brown 1978, 135). This has happened with North American liberation theologies rooted in the experiences of feminists, African-Americans, Native Americans, Latinos, Jews, and gays and lesbians. While Unitarian Universalism can draw from all of these sources, its heritage and current faith system place it in a unique position, separate from secular and religious liberation theologies, warranting a theology of liberation that speaks from and to its own context. In fashioning this new tradition, it can turn to its heritage, which, like Jewish Liberation Theology, is marked by ethics, the prophetic tradition, and the refusal of idolatry (Ellis 1989, 386).

Richard Gilbert gives expression to the Unitarian Universalist ethical tradition when he states:

...."reverence for life" is the ordering principle for a liberal religious social ethic, that reverence for life gives rise to a moral imperative to expand the quality of life through pursuit of love in interpersonal relationships, justice in social relationships, and trusteeship in our relationships with the non-human environment. *(Gilbert 1980, 97)*

Reverence for life was the dominant theme of Albert Schweitzer's philosophy[2] and it is an essential thread holding together the U.U.A.'s "Principles and Purposes" (UUA 1984).

Merely sitting by and watching, expecting our reverence for life to change the plight of the poor, would not be consistent with our prophetic tradition. A commitment to action is called for. James Luther Adams writes:

A group that does not concern itself with the struggle in history for human decency and justice, an expert who does not show concern for the shape of things to come, a church that does not attempt to interpret the signs of the times, is not prophetic. They are but representations of the past. We have long held to the idea of the priesthood of all believers....we need also a firm belief in the prophethood of all believers. The prophetic forces in society will appear where people think and work together to interpret the signs of the times in light of their faith, to make explicit through discussion the epochal thinking that the times demand. They will arise wherever it becomes a responsibility to attempt to forsee and foretell the consequences of human behavior and whenever there is the intention of participating in the creative dimensions of the future in place of merely being dragged into it. *(Adams, 32)*

The sense of empowerment and hope that comes with this prophethood, of creating history instead of being pushed by it, is critical in our move toward the poor.

Finally, a goal of liberation theology is humanization. One obstacle to achieving this is idolatry: the major theological struggle today is not between theism and atheism, but between theism and idolatry. Adams comments on this: "Liberalism in its generalized form has been the chief critic of the idolatries of creedalism, of church or political authoritarianism, of nationalistic, racial, or sexual chauvinism..." (Adams, 10). The humanization of society by religion must eliminate all idols rather than replace them with symbols that only substitute one form of idolatry for another. While liberalism has helped to eradicate idols, it also comes close to a danger:

> ....in its specialized form [liberalism] has generated a new form of idolatry, the idolatry of "possessive individualism." This possessive individualism has served as a smokescreen, an ideology, concealing or protecting a new authoritarianism of corporate economic power. This idolatry in the name of individualism and the "free market" eschews responsibility for the social consequences of economic power - it has become virtually unaccountable to the general public. (*Adams 10*)

Individualism helps in the creation of the poor who have been marginalized and isolated to the extreme. Individualism has emerged as a philosophy that isolates the person first by principle then by action. Therefore, individualism must be overcome.

The task, then, of a Unitarian Universalist Theology of Liberation is "to join with others in the ongoing struggle for human dignity and justice with the hope that we can become what we are called to be...." (Ellis 1989, 386). Ours must not only be a faith built on ethics with a prophetic tradition, but a faith that refuses idolatry. Liberation from the idolatry of "possessive individualism" is the next step. Without this idolatry, we would be free to move on in an exploration of our faith from the liberationist perspective. Liberating religious individualism is next on the agenda in seeking the creation of a Unitarian Universalist Liberation Theology.

Chapter Two

LIBERATING RELIGIOUS INDIVIDUALISM

LIBERATING RELIGIOUS INDIVIDUALISM

Individualism lies at the very core of American culture.

Robert Bellah

The scene is as recurrent and predictable as a New England Town Meeting. The issue is not as important as is the characterization of the debate. At this Congregational Meeting as at most others, the arguments will reflect an ardent, uncompromising belief in individualism.

The topic under debate was banning smoking in the church building. The first several people to speak suggested that the reality was smoking is bad - for the smoker as well as those in the area: it simply did not make sense to smoke. Another person rose to say that whether it was good or bad, smokers had the responsibility to go along with the group, whatever the vote might be (she was assuming a ban!).

Finally, some of the opposition spoke - none of them being smokers: "I want to defend the right of those who do smoke, to smoke," one of them said. "Since when have we been in the business of telling people what they can and cannot do!" There was some applause and then another supporter of smokers' rights spoke: "We've always protected the rights of the person here and I don't want to start taking away those rights now. I don't like smoking either, but if allowing it is what will keep us free here, then I want the ban voted down." The debate continued for another 15 minutes and then the vote: 55 for the ban, 2 against. As with similar issues about fairness, the nature of the debate is the same.

This Congregational Meeting highlights three forms of

individualism. The first Bellah calls "biblical" (Bellah 1985, 142). Biblical individualism recognizes the needs of the individual, but there are times when every person has a religious (biblical) obligation to go along with the group. In a culture where we believe in the dignity and sacredness of the individual, biblical individualism attempts to soften this belief by appealing to a religious context. In the case of the smoking debate, "it's bad to smoke" is an agrument that implies immorality. To be a good person (a religious person) would be to help the group and do as they do. The second form is described as "civic" individualism and is characterized by the need to do what is best for the group. Civic individualism is another attempt to harness a rampant belief in individualism by placing the needs of the group over those of the individual and thereby contributing to the common good (which would include the individual). Finally Bellah describes "modern individualism." Composed of both utilitarian and expressive needs, it holds that the individual must always take precedence over the group, and only after careful consideration can group needs be met. This form of individualism has taken over contemporary American culture:

> There are both ideological and sociological reasons for the growing strength of modern individualism at the expense of the civic and biblical traditions. Modern individualism has pursued individual rights and individual autonomy in ever new realms *(Bellah, 143)*.

Although there appear to be conflicts between these forms of individualism, Bellah believes the differences have historically been sidestepped because at their core all three philosophies "stress the dignity and autonomy of the individual" (Bellah, 142). Paul King supports the same conclusion: "The appeal is not to the good old days but the good old traditions" (King, Maynard and Woodyard 1988, 5). But as classical and biblical forms of individualism have more recently acquiesced to the tenets of modern individualism, problems have emerged:

> The question is whether an individualism in which the

self has become the main form of reality can really be sustained. What is at issue is not simply whether self-contained individuals might withdraw from the public sphere to pursue purely private ends, but whether such individuals are capable of sustaining either public *or* private life. *(Bellah, 14)*

Bellah is not suggesting that we return to the civic and biblical traditions of individualism; they also are inadequate. Both embody forms of discrimination that are intolerable in today's society - sexism, racism and a loss of individual dignity as the demands of the group become greater and stronger. The result?

We face a profound impasse. Modern individualism seems to be producing a way of life that is neither individually nor socially viable, yet a return to traditional forms would be to return to intolerable discrimination and oppression. The question, then, is whether the older civic and biblical traditions have the capacity to reformulate themselves while simultaneously remaining faithful to their own deepest insights. *(Bellah, 144)*

King supports Bellah's conclusion: "... some of our deepest problems both as individuals and as a society are closely linked to our individualism" (Bellah, 142). But King asserts that Bellah's analysis is only as good as far as it goes (King, 6). It is not enough to expect an emerging new individualism or a heroism out of the old order. The strengths of classical, biblical, and modern individualism have characteristics that are appealing, but carry too many social liabilities. King describes a "heroism" that recognizes the value of individualism, yet has its roots in a social basis: he describes an individualism which will grow out of solving the "tri-lemma" facing the middle class. The "tri-lemma" consists of economic instability, decreasing power, and a feeling of estrangement. Results from the "tri-lemma" are seen in an economy that has left the middle class increasingly on a par with the working class and as vulnerable to poverty as those at the bottom of the economy. With moderate to low participation in business decisions, the middle class is left cooperating in the oppression of workers, the unemployed, and the poor. "Finally," King writes:

> ... our structural powerlessness as employees and our individualism create a sense of isolation and meaninglessness, of being unable to change either our vulnerability to or our cooperation in that oppression. *(King, 61)*

Only through a middle class social heroism will the "tri-lemma" and its effects be confronted. This involves more than a superficial or limited undertaking since the results of the "tri-lemma" are ingrained in the country's identity and revealed in consumerism, nationalism, and religion (King, 38).

First, consumerism has become a way of life for the American middle class. King asserts: "It was Marx who suggested that 'you are what you do.' We seem to have changed that into 'you are what you consume'" (King, 39). Second, nationalism is a source of identity and meaning. In particular, many Unitarian Universalists believe their religion is interdependent with the American experiment and experience.[3] Pluralism, democracy, and expansion, all of which have shaped the United States, have shaped liberal faith. And third, religion has been a middle class source of definition. Whether religious fundamentalism, orthodoxy, or liberalism, "...the problems and their resolutions are couched in individualistic terms" (King, 40).

The oppressive nature of the "tri-lemma" will increase and debilitate the middle class further as long as the middle class continues to be defined by consumerism, materialism, and religion. Not until the "tri-lemma" is solved will the middle class be free to choose a way of life, identity, and meaning that will stand for justice and community in the biblical and classical traditions, yet free from the oppressive and discriminatory values associated with these heritages. The three forms of individualism critiqued by Bellah, and the three sources of identity put forward by King, are oppressive and isolating. There is nothing about them that promotes liberation, community-building, empowerment, and interdependency.

The Town Meeting and the congregational meeting are

examples of the pseudo-power King found in middle class communities. After the smoking debate at the Congregational Meeting, a member expressed his enthusiasm for what he heard: "Wasn't it great! We have such a variety of people here, such interesting ideas." His remarks add to a commonly expressed belief found in Unitarian Universalist congregations: they have become sanctuaries for religious eclecticism. This perspective is summarized by many who repeat: "You can believe anything and be a Unitarian!" (We are the Church of the Ten Suggestions). The notion is a correct one in this sense: We embrace all three forms of individualism as suggested by Bellah.[4] Both Bellah and King conclude that for American society, this embrace has created an impasse. It also has created an impasse for Unitarian Universalism. Unitarian Universalist church members can no longer take the mall approach: "We are like addictive mall shoppers who hope that one of their purchases will finally establish who they really are" (King, 183). Purchasing several forms of individualism, even all of them, as our identity, Unitarian Universalists have avoided making a critical decision, a decision that will have a profound impact on the future. We must decide. How will we decide?

Individualism as Ideology and Myth

"The inherent worth and dignity of every person" (UUA 1984) is sacrosanct in Unitarian Universalism. To suggest that the needs of the group are as valid as those of the individual (let alone more valid) is to prompt an inevitable look of disapproval if not outright hostility.[5] In some circles it results in the typical (and American) accusation of favoring socialism rather than a homeland version of democratic capitalism. While Bellah and others have explained the rise of individualism in American culture, Berger and Luckman provide a framework for understanding how individualism has reached near ontological and religious status (Berger and Luckmann 1966, 16).

Though integral to the faith of Unitarian Universalism, individualism is neither inherent nor ontological to Unitarian Universalism or American life. Individualism has achieved sacred-like status not because of a God-given character and quality, but due to the importance people give it. This ontological-like quality is achieved by a process called objectivation:

> It is important to keep in mind that the objectivity of the institutional world, however massive it may appear to the individual, is a humanly produced, constructed objectivity. The process by which the externalized products of human activity attain the character of objectivity is objectivation. *(Berger, 60)*

Understanding how the objectivation process works is not to suggest that individualism carries less value; it is to assert that its value is sacred because a person has chosen to make it sacred. In other words, though the world of experience might appear as objective reality, it cannot be separated from its origin - humans.

King says that objectivation is never value-free. The construction of social reality, that is, the meaning given to everything, is completed in a biased environment. But then, this is the nature of ideology:

> ... ideology refers to the evaluative use of ideas in defense of a particular position, representing only the interests of one contending group against another. It does not disclose historically valid knowledge, but conceals the fact that human beings have constructed reality. *(King, 101)*

All people have an ideology: "Let him who is without ideology cast the first stone" (Berryman 1987, 134). There is nothing wrong with this, it is the reality of everyday life. Individualism, as an ideology, cannot be condemned or devalued for these reasons. It is simply to say that as an ideology, individualism is embraced by Unitarian Universalists (and in all likelihood, by American culture) for good reasons. Individualism has achieved sacred status because it supports, encourages, and gives meaning to a particular way of life and system of faith - *we have decided to make it so.* As Unitarian Universalists and others have their faith in individualism, some faith traditions place their emphasis elsewhere, and it is done by objectivation. For example, Richard Shaull explains the belief and meaning of God like this: "God exists in us as we develop the right concepts" (Schaull 1984, 36). He is suggesting that through the process of objectivation, as certain ideas are developed and then projected outward, God is created.

There is no objective reality.[6] Individualism may appear as objective reality because it is such an integral part of the Unitarian Universalist faith system. The appearance of its ontological worth creates a closed circle or tautology preserving the status quo; an ideology and theology have been constructed that appear to be "something other than human" (Berger, 61).

The process does not stop here. Ideology embodied in the form of story is mythology. "Myths are central in human life," writes Alice Blair Wesley. She elaborates:

...All people and cultures without exception hold myths to be true. Any who believe that others - less sophisticated - may naively hold myths to be true while they themselves do not, are themselves naive. *(Wesley 1987, 20)*

Sam Keen expands on this: "... myth refers to interlocking stories, rituals, rites, customs and beliefs that give a pivotal sense of meaning and direction to a person, a family, a community or a culture" (Keen 1988, 44).

As myth, the objectivation of reality, which has become ideology, can be retold, rehearsed, and re-presented repeatedly. As a myth, it can easily be passed on from generation to generation, giving it historical validity that in turn lends greater credence to its ontological-like character. Like ideology, mythology is deeply rooted and revealing: "....the myths we tell become who we are and what we believe...." (Keen, 44) As ideology supports and nurtures the status quo, so too does mythology. "A myth involves the conscious celebration of certain values," writes Keen:

....always personified in a pantheon of heroes....But it also includes an unconscious, habitual way of seeing things, an invisible stew of unquestioned assumptions.

29

A living myth, like an iceberg, is only 10 percent visible: 90 percent lies beneath the surface of consciousness of those who live by it. *(Keen, 44)*

Mythology is powerful, but not permanent. Individualism as an ideology for Unitarian Universalism is integral to the faith message and tradition, but it is not absolute. It is there because we have placed it there and we continue to tell the myths that bolster, perpetuate, and give meaning to Unitarian Universalist individualism. At the same time that Unitarian Universalists tell the myths of individualism, we also talk about pluralism, another integral element of our faith.

This Is Pluralism?

Pluralism is a goal and ideal which Americans affirm and aspire to; it is a principle that Unitarian Universalists agree is not only commendable, but desirable. Pluralism is a condition that is central to American democracy and the nation's self image, and the Unitarian Universalist Association's (UUA) heritage and corporate conception. It is written in the UUA's "Principles and Purposes:" "We affirm and promote the inherent worth and dignity of every person ... acceptance of one another ... respect for the interdependent web of all existence of which we are a part" (UUA 1984).

Pluralism refers to differences among people that are tolerated without loss of individual or group character. Pluralism means that every person has a right to participate on every level of societal life regardless of who they are and what they think. Pluralism in religion means diversity of people and thought all under the same name. In both the nation and Unitarian Universalism, pluralism exists when there is no attempt to declare one person, belief, or way of life better than another; if your skin color or faith are not like the majority of citizens you are not less American or less religious. In other words, pluralism, in nation and religion, is the recognition that there are differences among people and this is all right. Indeed, pluralism is to be celebrated.

Pluralism is not the antithesis of individualism, pluralism supports individualism. The pluralism and diversity that are proclaimed as integral to the Unitarian Universalist faith are based on respect for the inherent worth and dignity of every person. But what standard is being used to determine these? What is the context of understanding? Consider the changing diversity of the international religious community: Christianity, Buddhism, and Judaism are losing followers while Islam and Hinduism are increasing. Also significant is that since 1900, the number of nonreligious and atheists have increased by over 20 percent (Hodgson 1988, 93). Peter Hodgson concludes:

> The world reality reflected by these figures may only with difficulty sink into the consciousness of a nation at present experiencing an evangelical revival. But in light of the numbers it is not entirely inappropriate to ask whether religion as such is destined gradually to become a "thing of the past" for human consciousness, as life becomes increasingly technological, instrumental, and secular in its orientation, ideology, skills and values. *(Hodgson, 93)*

In the United States, all minorities are increasing: Latinos number the largest, changing forever the North Atlantic look of the nation. With each year, the U.S. becomes less North Atlantic and the bond of one language slowly diminishes. The U.S. now has a diversity of cultures unparalleled in its past. The diversity has been a result of rising immigration from Latin America and Asia, in addition to immigrants from Eastern Europe and the Middle East. The result? "... some Americans who were born in the United States are saying they cannot identify with its prevailing culture" (Hacker 1990, 19).

As diversity gains momentum on all levels, responses in local communities aren't good: racism, sexism, and homophobia are at dramatically high levels; the rich and poor grow further apart; there seems to be a strengthening of individual self-protection and isolation. Against this backdrop of a rapidly growing and changing population,

Judith Waldrop asks: "Did you know that only about one in 1,000 Americans who belong to a church or synagogue is a Unitarian Universalist?" (Waldrop 1988, 11)

As diversity races ahead, what about pluralism? What about respect and welcoming of individual differences? As a nation and as a religious movement, there is the possibility that we will find ourselves on the wrong side of history because we are not prepared for the changes taking place. We do not see clearly the diverse patterns in the social order, we've closed our eyes and ears to the desire for pluralism. Unitarian Universalist church historian Conrad Wright says about the need to respond:

> Liberal religion articulated a value system that derived its strength from the social arrangements made possible by the discovery of the exploitable resources of the New World. But those resources were not limitless. The infinity of the private individual was plausible enough on the shores of Walden Pond, when there was no one closer than Concord Village a mile away; it is hollow rhetoric on the streets of Calcutta or in the barrios of Caracas. The progress of humankind onward and upward forever may have seemed an axiom grounded in history to James Freeman Clarke; it seems something less than that to the residents of Middletown, Pennsylvania. The principle of religious toleration was easy for Jefferson, who could not see that it did any injury for his neighbor to say there are twenty gods or no god; but the principles of toleration takes on a sharper edge when the decisive differences are not in the realm of speculative theology, but on the question of apartheid and what it is that others should be forced, despite their opinions, to do about it. *(Wright 1989, 164)*

Moving Toward Liberation

Latin American Liberation Theology gives Unitarian Universalists one way to move toward pluralism as a living myth. Here is an opportunity to embrace a faith that liberates *for* the needs of the group, an individualism that combines the best of the civic and biblical traditions while keeping in balance the demands of modern individualism.

32

The issues of liberation *for* will be highlighted elsewhere. Now it is important to understand from what we are being liberated, what the Boff brothers refer to as "pre-theology" (Boff 1987, 22). In other words, why liberation?

We need liberation because we are increasingly empty. Erich Fromm said: "....much of what we do is an attempt to keep ourselves from fully acknowledging our boredom" (Fromm 1986, 14). Charles Bayer refers to a "spiritual ennui" (Bayer 1986, 60) that he believes has become commonplace in American culture. With the routine of the daily work world and personal calendars that reflect every waking moment planned, many Americans settle into bed at night feeling exhausted and empty. Bayer supports Fromm's assertion:

> Perhaps to a greater degree than any mass culture in history, affluent U.S. middle-class folk have more spare time and more money to use, as they please, but little they can do, no place they can go and nothing they can buy seems to fill the gray void. *(Bayer, 60)*

It is no wonder that our churches have more members claiming that their lives are empty, meaningless - they feel a dark hole, a hole that can't be lighted or filled. They turn to the church looking for fulfillment, they want to be handed the meaning of life just as one might go to the supermarket to be handed packaged meat.

Not finding their needs met by an inner strength, some turn to alternatives - work, relationships, alcohol, drugs. These are the most common choices. These all help to make up the co-dependencies that have taken over many lives. Some churches support the work of self-help programs: here are opportunities for a handful who have had the courage to face their reality. They gather with other co-dependents to share their experiences and together they nurture one another on the road back to recovery.

Another interrelated issue to spiritual ennui is a life without risk or adventure. Not that one must sign up for adventures in Outward Bound or run a marathon, but just to be moved by life, to be passionate about living and compassionate for those with whom one lives. Life is often structured in such a way that won't allow for the adventurous, the impromptu, or even the unthought-of. Following the death of a parishioner, David Rankin was moved to write:

> A religion that promises a life without tension, a life without conflict, life without suffering - is a religion of passivity, a religion of mediocrity, a religion of insignificance. Besides, everything worth doing in the world is a desperate gamble, a game of chance, where nothing is certain. *(Rankin 1978, 29)*

Spiritual ennui in the forms of boredom, codependency, and a lack of adventure dominate the lives of middle class church members. Liberation from these dehumanizing forces would free people to place their energies outside of themselves. But in order to make this final step, a step away from the isolation supported and nurtured by modern individualism, there has to be a recognition that this destructive individualism is hurting people and through them, their churches.

This is not to say that individualism *per se* is bad. What is desired is pluralism. Pluralism embraces the inherent worth and dignity of every person - pluralism celebrates individualism. But Unitarian Universalism is not pluralistic. Quite the opposite is the case: "Unitarian Universalists are well educated with 95% having attained a college degree and over 1/4 having graduate degrees; we are economically secure with 70% earning over $30,000 a year and 1 in 3 taking home over $50,000; we are 98% white. The figures are just as revealing when you look at our values, entertainment, politics, even the magazines we read and the cars we drive" (Waldrop 1988, 12). We are anything but pluralistic: the membership of Unitarian Universalism is dramatically homogeneous. In short, our churches are not the environments we thought. Given this homogeneity, there is little reason to believe that "....we go to church to stand over-against ourselves and pull ourselves into the hard truths of our existence" (Thandeka 1989, 46), the kind of pulling that might liberate us from the orthodoxies of personal and social forces that prevent achieving a life of value and meaning.

The discrepancy of myth and ideology with reality and the ideal might, at first, be sobering, even frightening. Moving beyond homogeneity will not be easy, but it will liberate to a pluralism that could evoke a new myth, an accurate mythology. Perhaps the creation of a new story is the risk and adventure needed. King suggests it is: "Theology is most vital and creative when a community begins to recognize that its conception of the world and the actual conditions of historical existence are at odds" (King, 145).

If we will take notice, this is exactly what is happening to us. The Unitarian Universalist myth of individualism is antiquated and losing strength - it is not facing up to reality, but instead, it is supporting its followers in lifestyles that are destructive to themselves, their communities, and the world. As life around us moves forward at breakneck speed, as personal lives are slipping away, can liberal faith keep up? Wright concludes:

> So the fate of religious liberalism rests with us. We may cling to the old paradigm, proclaim individual freedom of belief as an absolute value ... Then we may dwindle in numbers and influence until we end up a museum piece, like the Shakers, the Schwenkfelders, and the Swedenborgians. But on the other hand, we may learn how to relate to new social forces, to master a new paradigm. If so, we may not simply assure our own survival as a segment of the Church Universal, but we may even contribute something to the humanizing of what threatens to be a far less comfortable world than the one you and I have known. *(Wright, 166)*

The time is now to study and critique what Unitarian Universalism stands for; to explore the changes and patterns that keep pace around us; to dream, articulate, plan, and implement the future course.

Chapter Three

TOWARD A UNITARIAN UNIVERSALIST
THEOLOGY OF LIBERATION

TOWARD A UNITARIAN UNIVERSALIST THEOLOGY OF LIBERATION

We are not to edit a North American edition of Latin American theology, but to create a new version of North American theology.

Robert McAfee Brown

The development of a Unitarian Universalist Theology of Liberation resembles the theological shift that some are seeking (McFague 1991), a shift that recognizes the needs, concerns, and hopes reflective of the diversity and pluralism found in the community of life. My awareness of the need for this shift was glaring during a seminary class discussion.

A minister from a small rural church located in a town on the Chesapeake Bay described his town's unemployment rate, which was very high among the African-American members of his church. Similar to conditions in other small Bay towns, they too were suffering from a rapidly declining fishing industry being blamed on the Bay's pollution and resulting in economic devastation. Consequently, he was supporting the growth of new industry - it would mean new jobs for his people. The only obstacle standing in the way of these new jobs was an environmental coalition that was seeking an injunction to prevent the building of an industrial park on Bay wetlands. My colleague was outraged at this - not only was the coalition preventing badly needed jobs, but the coalition's membership was composed of white people living outside of the town.

Discussion followed his description. There were those who understood and supported his work. They spoke strongly about the need for human dignity and balancing economic power. Those speaking were African-Americans.

39

"But what about the destruction of the Bay?" was the reply from others: they cited Bay pollution as the cause of the problem from the beginning; they argued that the problem would not be solved by filling in the wetlands; this was only a temporary solution to be revisited again, perhaps in another town. A new awareness had to be created and stopping the proposed industrial park was the right place to start. Those speaking were white.

It was clear to me that both groups had something important to contribute to the debate, yet neither was willing to admit to the priorities of the other. I left the class torn over what appeared an unresolvable dilemma: economic justice versus environmental integrity, immediate need versus future stability, blacks versus whites - these were the more obvious issues involved. Ellie Goodwin gives voice to the dilemma:

> Environmentalists are among the first to lead a charge to save life or enhance its quality. The core of the argument between social activists and environmentalists is definition of "life" and what needs to be "preserved." It is one thing to talk about saving offshore birds and wetlands; it's a very different story to talk about saving an inner city child's life. When viewed in such terms, it is hard to come to any nexus that would allow creative collaboration. Yet the quality and preservation of habitats for both these life forms are crucial to their continued survival. The struggle to work towards that nexus - that point of mutual understanding - is at the center of the new environmentalism. *(Goodwin, 54)*

With hindsight, I see that the debate regarding jobs versus the environment reflects the urgent need for a shift in liberation thinking. Both arguments were correct: one could not be made at the exclusion of the other. What is now needed is a theology that speaks to both issues. The editors of *Liberating Life* give voice to this need:

> In our view, justice and sustainability must be united into a single vision of life-giving hope. Although the principles of justice and sustainability may be in tension in the structures of present society, social justice and ecological sustainability ultimately require one another.

There can be no justice without sustainability and no sustainability without justice. A society that seeks only justice without regard to the consequences of its behavior for the ecological future cannot be just. But it is equally true that a society which abandons concern for justice rides roughshod over the concerns of the poor and the powerless as well as the environment on which the continuance of life depends. *(Birch, Eakin and McDaniel 1990, 2)*

Birch, Eakin and McDaniel, in their *Liberating Life*, write of a theological breakthrough. The language of traditional liberation theology, as outlined in Chapter I, is theistic and Christological, a language that does not always speak to the Unitarian Universalist faith and context. Birch, Eakin and McDaniel emphasize the value of ecojustice needs. They broaden the liberation theology agenda and they increase the hope for an inclusive liberation language. By doing this, they widen the window of faith that enables faith traditions like Unitarian Universalism to join the struggle, which prior to now has not been possible.

In this chapter, using the language being forced by this theological shift and contextualized in Unitarian Universalism, I will point the way toward a Unitarian Universalist Theology of Liberation.

A Theological Shift

Contextualization is a cornerstone in the theology of the liberationist. All theology will not be the same because all contexts have to satisfy their own theological demands. This is the nature of praxis, the reflection-action-reflection-action process (see page 5). Inherent to this process is a pragmatism that places a high value on theology: it demands support for the faith system - if it cannot support and nurture life, it must be held accountable, if not altered. Sallie McFague suggests that this is reason enough to urge an examination of the Christian tradition:

No matter how ancient a metaphorical tradition may be and regardless of its credentials in scripture, liturgy, and creedal statements, it still must be discarded if it threatens the continuation of life itself. If the heart of the

Christian gospel is the salvific power of God, triumphalist metaphors cannot express that reality *in our time*, whatever their appropriateness may have been in the past. *(McFague 1990, 211)*

McFague encourages a shift to signal a new theological agenda, a shift marked by three changes (McFague 1991, 14 -15). The first change will result from challenges to dualistic thinking, a mode of thought that has come to characterize not only theology, but Western life. She says:

In whatever ways we might reconstruct the symbols of God, human being and earth, this can no longer be done in a dualistic fashion, for the heavens and the earth are *one* phenomenon, albeit an incredibly ancient, rich and varied one. *(McFague 1991, 14)*

McFague is suggesting that despite its richness and its ancient origins, the image of God and humanity, as two separate realities, is no longer meaningful. What is needed are images and symbols that reflect the unity of the divine and human. Hierarchies must be abandoned. This would encourage developing an inclusive, cosmocentric theology. The pluralism supporting this shift reflects the shared life held as common by all on earth (as earthlings). It also reflects the reality of individual differences, the uniqueness of everything on earth (as in pluralism).

The second shift will be characterized by a commitment to consequences:

....it insists that one of the criteria of constructive theological reflection - thinking about our place in the earth and the earth's relation to its source - is a concern with the consequences of proposed constructions for those who live within them. *(McFague 1991, 15)*

Theology in the academy has traditionally been scholarly and objective, and in this sense distant from the laity: it has been a view of society from the top looking down. The academy's theological interpretation has been a functional one whereby the relationships and mechanics of society are best when operating harmoniously, when conflicts are viewed as maladjustments best resolved by conflict resolution (Bonino 1983, 46). From this persepctive, order is the prevailing mindset of the academician. But as Jose Bonino suggests, justice (freedom from oppression) does not come from the top down, with a view toward harmony and order (Bonino 1983, 84-86). For Bonino, the scholarly theological approach is unconcerned with "the consequences of proposed constructions for those who live within them."

Liberation theology, as a "theology from below," is dialectical. Society is not viewed from the top down, but from the perspective of those who live with the consequences, with the conflicts. A dialectical understanding of society looks at the complex intricacies and doesn't set out to create or impose order and harmony. Instead, it seeks "to understand the structural basis and dynamics of such conflicts" (Bonino 1983, 46). A dialectical approach to theology preserves scholarly commitment while also paying attention to consequences. A commitment to consequences, the second characteristic of the shift, demonstrates that "theological reflection is a *concerned* affair, concerned that this constructive thinking be on the side or the well-being of the planet and all its creatures" (McFague 1991, 15).

The last change will be characterized by the abandonment of idolatry. Anthropocentrism and other dualisms have contributed to an idolatrous attitude that has created oppression and destruction of earth and its life. Abandoning idolatry is critical to liberation:

> The refusal to be idolatrous is the refusal to place systems of domination over the human quest for compassion and solidarity. Stated another way, Christian liberation theologians assert that the God we worship is not defined by the prayers we say or the words used to justify activities in the world, but that the activity itself defines our God and commitment. When we face a system of domination whose rationale assumes a transcendent quality, the only honest response is to refuse to "worship" or participate in that system. Thus the refusal to be idolatrous can be seen as the willingness to be a-theistic. The question of idolatry, then, often does not begin with

43

affirming transcendence but with breaking away from a false transcendence which legitimates oppression. Idolatry distorts judgment; breaking with idolatry opens the possibility of clarity and justice. *(Ellis 1987, 89-90)*

Classroom understanding of conflicts and consequences will not be enough. Responsibility and commitment will characterize this paradigm shift, the kind that has already been witnessed in the politics of the Green Movement where the spiritual dimensions of refusing idolatrous worship have been politicized (Spretnak 1986, 45-69).[7]

Abandoning dualistic thinking, focusing on consequences, and taking seriously a commitment to breaking the oppressive systems that have destroyed earth, these three will characterize a theological paradigm shift: the shift will broaden the scope of traditional liberation concerns and create a more inclusive base of support among all faith traditions, including Unitarian Universalism. The style or approach of theological reflection used in the shift must by necessity be a bold and assertive one. The patterns, stereotypes, images, and myths to be recreated are deeply ingrained in our thinking and living. By pushing the boundaries of conventional academic theology, a paradigm shift will take the risk of giving voice to what had only been thought; it must seek to challenge the assumptions of accepted creeds and speak with authority to unquestioned policies; it must fill the silence left by the oppressed and ignored members of creation who are unable to voice their rights as earthlings. McFague calls this heuristic theology:

> Thus heuristic theology will be one that experiments and tests, that thinks in an as-if fashion, that imagines possibilities that are novel, that dares to think differently....
>
> Its experimental character means it is a kind of theology well suited for times of uncertainty and change, when systematic, comprehensive construction seems inappropriate if not impossible. It could be "free theology," for it must be willing to play with possibilities and, as a consequence, not take itself too seriously, accepting its tentative, relative, partial, and hypothetical character. *(McFague 1990, 205-206)*

Welcoming the characteristics of a theological shift and encouraged by the broadness and support of a heuristic or free theology, I will now turn to a consideration of some central liberation themes and what they might look like in a Unitarian Universalist context. These themes will be God, poverty, Reign of God, and God's preferential option for the poor.

God

Birch writes that there are three views of the relationship between creation and God (Birch 1990, 194). One is classical theism, which separates God from creation in all ways. Another view of the God-creation relation is: "God is involved in the cosmos but is not identified with it. God is both within the system and independent of it. This is panentheism" (Birch 1990, 194).[8] Breaking away from traditional hierarchial characterizations of God (classical theism) or less orthodox views (panentheism) is critical to Christian theology and it is essential in the development of a Unitarian Universalist Theology of Liberation. As a creedless and dogma-free faith, a liberal faith, Unitarian Universalists would question such traditional characterizations and would probably refrain from using the word God simply because of the orthodox and oppressive associations made with it (as Adams suggested, see page 9). In its "Principles and Purposes," Unitarian Universalism affirms "the interdependent web of all existence of which we are part (UUA 1984). Inasmuch, there is a third view that says that God is the creation, inseparable from it. This is pantheism. McFague spells out the implications:

> Our nuclear knowledge brings to the surface a fundamental fact about human existence. We are part and parcel of the web of life and exist in interdependence with all other beings, both human and nonhuman. As Pierre Teilhard de Chardin puts it in a moment of insight: "I realized that my own poor trifling existence was one with the immensity of all that is and all that is in the process of becoming." Or, as the poet Wallace Stevens says, "Nothing is itself taken alone. Things are because of interrelations and interconnections." The evolutionary, ecological perspective insists that we are, in the

most profound way, "not our own": we belong, from the cells of our bodies to the finest creations of our minds, to the intricate, ever-changing cosmos. We both depend on that web of life for our own continued existence and in a special way we are responsible for it, for *we alone know* that life is interrelated and *we alone know* how to destroy it. It is an awesome - and unsettling - thought. *(McFague 1990, 202)*

Clearly, McFague stresses the importance of "the interdependent web" relationship of life. Yet as an outspoken critic of orthodoxy and as a leader in heuristic theology, she falls one step short of going the distance. "We belong to the cosmos," she writes. We depend on the web for our existence; everything is interrelated, nothing is separate from the other. McFague is speaking the language of ontology. We can't get more basic and elementary than she has. She defines the terms of our life sustenance, the ground of our being, as the cosmos. We are *of* the cosmos, we *are* the cosmos. The two are inseparable. Is it too radical to suggest, then, that God and the Cosmos are synonymous, they are indistinguishable, one and the same? I don't believe it is, it makes a great deal of sense. John Mbiti says more:

....this is a religious universe. Nature in the broadest sense of the word is not an empty impersonal object or phenomenon; it is filled with religious significance.... The physical and spiritual are but two dimensions of one and the same universe. These dimensions dovetail into each other to the extent that at times and in places one is apparently more real than, but not exclusive of, the other. *(Sindima 1990, 143)*

Mbiti lends further support to an inescapable reality: Cosmos as God and God as Cosmos will be interchangeable in a Unitarian Universalist Liberation Theology. All life is sacred because life is of the Cosmos, is God. Harvey Sindima provides an excellent description:

Moyo is the Malawian word for such life. *Moyo*, written with a lower case *m,* is both physical and spiritual. In

part, *moyo*, is life as it is manifested in biological existence. As such it is shared by, and bonds together, all
living things. But *moyo* is also spiritual and sacred: even
moyo as it is manifested in biological existence is rooted
in the Mystery. Divine life, signified by the capitalized
Moyo , is the source and foundation of all *moyo* . All life -
that of people, plants and animals, and the earth - originates from and therefore shares an intimate relationship
of bondedness with divine life; all life is divine life. *(Sindima 1990, 144)*

Sindima comes closer than does McFague but still does
not claim God as synonymous with the Cosmos. Why this
reluctance? I can think of two reasons: First, McFague and
Sindima might believe that God as Cosmos diminishes the
stature of God and whatever associations go with it. This
is trying to keep hold of traditional past characterizations,
precisely what McFague and others have tried to shake
free from. Using the language of panentheism as a means
of separating God and cosmos is too confusing ("God is involved in the cosmos but is not identified with it. God is
both within the system and independent of it." Birch 1990,
194) and for Unitarian Universalists, among others, recalls
the confusion of the trinitarian three-in-one characterization. It also falls short of the clarity sought by free theology.

Second, Sindima, as does McFague (McFague 1990,
214, 217), gives nature high prominence. He might not
want construed from this assertion that nature's destruction and/or the destruction of the Cosmos would mean the
destruction of God. But how can God be destroyed? How
can the Cosmos be destroyed? It cannot.

McFague doesn't carry to its logical conclusion her
own idea:

....we are part of the cosmos where the cosmos itself has
come to consciousness. If we become extinct, then the
cosmos will lose its human, although presumably not its
divine, consciousness. As Jonathan Schell remarks, "In
extinction a darkness falls over the world not because
the lights have gone out but because the eyes that behold
the light have been closed." *(McFague 1990, 214)*

The Cosmos as God is never-ending, with or without the life forms that compose its web of existence. There can be no destruction of the Cosmos, there is no risk of destruction - it is life producing, nurturing, and sustaining despite humans. This is the logical conclusion of McFague's argument. Her argument does not result in classical theism, nor panentheism; God is not separate from creation nor is God a two-in-one formula. God is the Cosmos.

As part of the Cosmos, we are its consciousness. As its consciousness, we must act *as if* we are "the ultimate valuator or the ultimate agent in human history or both" (Jones 1973, xxii). This is not contradictory of the need to escape anthropocentric dualism. Isn't this the reality we must live with? Here is the awesome responsibility McFague refers to above. Decisions are not made to benefit humankind alone (anthropocentrism) or those with the most power (oppression): decisions are made interdependent with the processes of the Cosmos, which are deciphered by both simple observation (common sense) and scientific study. As theology, this has been called ecological theology (Birch, Eakin, McDaniel, 1990). As politics, these ideas are incorporated in the Green Movement:

> The Green principle of ecological wisdom always occupies the primary position because it means far more than mere environmentalism or saving what's left. The Greens have in mind deep ecology. Deep ecology encompasses the study of Nature's subtle web of interrelated processes and the application of that study to our interactions with Nature and among ourselves. Principles of deep ecology are that the well-being and flourishing of human and nonhuman life on earth have inherent value, that richness and diversity of life forms contribute to the realization of these values and are also values in themselves, and that humans have no right to reduce this richness and diversity except to satisfy vital needs. Human systems may take from Nature lessons concerning interdependence, diversity, openness to change within a system, flexibility, and the ability to adapt to new events or conditions outside the system. *(Spretnak, 23-24)*

The suggestion that God and the Cosmos are synonymous is not a new idea. But given the escalating ecological and political injustices of recent decades, there is a need for a broader, more inclusive liberation theology. The picture of God as Cosmos is one of wholeness and interdependency. This image plays a role of critical importance as we come to terms with the reductionistic and dualistic attitudes and actions that oppress life. McFague, using the metaphor of the cosmos as God's body, summarizes what is at stake, a summary that would be as valid when used with the God as Cosmos image:

> We see through pictures. We do not see directly. The pictures of a king and his realm and of the world as God's body are ways of speaking, ways of imagining the God-world relationship. The one pictures a vast distance between God and the world; the other imagines them as instrinsically related. At the close of day one asks which distortion (assuming that all pictures are false in some respects) is better by asking what attitudes each encourages. This is not the first question to ask, but it may well be the last. The monarchial model encourages attitudes of militarism, dualism, and escapism; it has nothing to say about the nonhuman world. The model of the world as God's body encourages holistic attitudes of responsibility for and care of the vulnerable and oppressed; it is nonhierarchial and acts through persuasion and attraction; it has a great deal to say about the body and nature. Both are pictures. Which distortion is more true to the world in which we live....? *(McFague 1990, 218)*

For Unitarian Universalists (and I hope for others), the Cosmos as God is an image, description, and reality true of the world in which we live. Cosmos as God can become a critical theme in the development of a Unitarian Universalist Theology of Liberation because it allows for a wholistic, interdependent, inclusive understanding and interpretation. With this understanding, Unitarian Universalists can enter the liberation dialogue.

Theodicy and Poverty

Suffering is integral to liberation theology. Suffering that results from the prevention or loss of humanization is a form of poverty (often resulting from no economic power) and is the reason for liberation theology (Gutierrez 1973, 288-291). Vieth says: "Suffering is a state of severe stress occurring when a person or people perceive their intactness or wholeness to be endangered by pain, injury, loss or oppression" (Vieth 1988, 11).

Suffering is personal. When humanization is blocked and oppression is experienced as a group (due to membership in a nation, community, or due to ethnicity (Jones 1989)), the impact is felt individually. Liberation theology, therefore, must confront the issue of theodicy. Jones writes: "The theologian or philosopher of liberation *must* engage in the enterprise of theodicy if he is to accomplish his task" (Jones 1973, xx).

As with its orthodox and parochial predecessors, the traditional focus of liberation theology has been anthropocentric issues: poverty and suffering have been exclusively humankind's. This makes sense given theology's cultural and historical emphasis, especialy in the academy: What else could compete with humankind as cosmic consciousness? In order to determine and alleviate the causes of poverty and suffering, thinking in dualistic and hierarchial fashions that place humankind on top or in the center cannot continue. With knowledge from the past balanced by current unerstanding, the oppressive and destructive results of anthropocentrism (or humanocentrism) can be altered. Liberation theology, then, must be broadened in two ways.

First, human liberation must be viewed interdependent with the Cosmos. In the Cosmocentric (or ecocentric) framework, humankind's suffering is a priority. As its consciousness, the oppression from dehumanization cannot be dismissed; as members of the Cosmos, all humans are divine creatures. But interdepdency also means that the needs of humankind cannot be satisfied at the exclusion or neglect of other life forms. Suffering occurs not because the Cosmos wills it, seeks it, or chooses pain; poverty, in all its forms (e.g., economic, spiritual, or emotional), is part of Life's repertoire of responses initiated by humankind's neglect - from our abuse of each other and the Cosmos. The processes of sustainability are inherent in the Cosmos. It is life giving. It is also life taking. The Cosmos is.

Second, an ecocentric theology of liberation must elevate those values which traditional liberation theologies have ignored. This ignorance has supported spiritual and emotional poverty and suffering. For example, traditional liberationists have fallen short by using radical socio-economic theories as a form of self-legitimation. Economic sensitivity should not be abandoned, but it must be placed in a better perspective. Gregory Baum describes liberation theology at its best, a description that characterizes the concerns of Cosmocentric Liberation Theology:

> The reason that social thinkers and political scientists are so fascinated by liberation theology is that here they see a social theory of the left that gives those who struggle a tremendous sense of identity and community. Liberation theology does not say to the people, you have nothing to lose but your chains. It assures them, on the contrary, that they have inherited a religious tradition that is the bearer of radical values. Liberation theology gives them an extraordinary sense of historical continuity, reaching back to the exodus community whom God delivered from oppression in the land of bondage. *(Baum 1989, 222)*

Also, some liberation theologies have turned to scientific empiricism. They claim clarity as their justification. "But," writes Haught, "this method deliberately leaves so much out (such as considerations of value, beauty, and purpose)" (Haught 1990, 162). With both scientific empiricism and socio-economic theory, different versions of the same approach, the strengths of an ecocentric, Cosmocentric Liberation Theology are ignored, and the suffering and poverty that has characterized anthropocentrism continues to flourish and oppress. Haught concludes:

> The disdain for mystery implied in these two intimately

connected standards of exploration has dramatically negative implications for how we regard the natural world in a scientific age. Even though initially the quest for clarity and simplicity seems innocent enough, unless carefully contained it can become a weapon of power wielded ruthlessly to hack away the rich undergrowth of vagueness that goes along with any cherishing of mystery....Thus to the extent that an environmental ethic would have to grow out of at least some appreciation and reverence for the mystery of nature, modern ideals of clear and exhaustive explanation can easily prove deleterious if they overrun their legitimate espistemological margins....What it requires now is the development of a new mystique of nature that does not reject the subject and history, but places them in a cosmic setting. *(Haught 1990, 163)*

The Preferential Option for the Poor

"A new mystique of nature" is found when reshaping the liberation theme of God's preferential option for the poor. Herzog writes:

...Our identity lies with what God does in taking sides with losers. They have no one but God to stand up for them. This basic social location is equally important for our relationship with creation. Only those who understand the underside of history can sense the underside of nature - "the groaning of creation" (Rom. 8:22). *(Herzog 1988, 41)*

The essence of the Cosmos is life-giving and life-sustaining: it provides for life, both human and nonhuman. In this sense, then, the enchancement of living (e.g., humanization) is an objective in a Cosmocentric Theology of Liberation; it is an objective nurtured by balance and limit. Inherent to the Cosmocentric process is balance, which only now we are beginning to understand. Cosmic balance is maintained and characterized by limits. Only with balance and limits can the integrity of the Cosmos remain intact. Hedstrom concludes:

....the idea of balance and environmental limits offers the

prospect of a more just society. This is because respect for these limits is essential to any social body that aspires to a qualitatively better life for all. Traditional industrial society, as we know, has not really presented us with this possibility.

In other words, we must develop a new ethic and, to be frank, a new logic with relation to nature, based on the conviction, as Father Gustavo Gutierrez of Peru says, "life and not death has the last word." We rightly insist that God opposes death because God is the Creator and the giver of life." *(Hedstrom 1990, 121)*

What kind of a God would choose to "side" with the poor? Just what does this mean? Berryman answers: "....the point is not that God is on the side of the guerilla groups, but that God is on the side of the poor and that what is at stake in the life of the poor is not simply an ethical exigency but the very nature of God" (Berryman 1984, 380).

While Berryman offers a clearer understanding of the preferrential option concept, asserting that God is on one side or another creates divisions that don't exist. Berryman and others use the wrong language - needless and divisive language. God, as Cosmos, just is.

To speak of *God's* preferential option for the poor is to work for balance while recognizing limits, which is the nature of the Cosmos (which is God). The Cosmos, as God, provides for all. The Cosmos has an essence, which is to sustain itself. Whoever (whatever) does not work interdependently with the Cosmos, is working against it. As parts of this Cosmos, living members of the interdependent web, human beings are elements of its life sustenance. From a liberation perspective, dehumanization occurs because of theo-ethical oppression. This is an abuse of humanity and a denial to life; it is also an act against the Cosmos, against God. Acting on behalf of the oppressed, the poor, is choosing to work for the life-giving and life-sustaining power of the Cosmos; acting for the oppressed, the poor, is working for balance within limits. Reshaping the preferential option theme of Latin American Liberation Theology results in a broader, more inclusive language. Hedstrom performs this task:

> In light of this ravaging of people and land in Central America, we realize that the preferential option for the poor, characteristic of Latin American liberation theologies, must be articulated as a preferential *option for life.* To exercise this option is to defend and promote the fundamental right to life of *all* creatures on earth. The right to life in all its fullness involves partaking of the material base of creation, that is, of the material goods that permit life. All people, and not the powerful alone, must be availed of such goods; all people, not the powerful alone, must do so in a way that preserves rather than despoils the earth and other forms of life. *(Hedstrom, 121)*

A Cosmocentric preferential option for life means choosing balance and limits (the nature of the Cosmos). The fullness of life can then be shared by all. An alternative perspective suggests that sharing occurs because what suffering exists is distributed evenly (Jones 1973, 21): suffering doesn't result from oppression, but for reasons other than abuse and neglect of the Cosmos (e.g., disease or natural disaster).

As members of the North Atlantic community, Unitarian Universalists (and others) are in a unique position. Largely white, well educated, and financially secure (this is to say, socially comfortable), Unitarian Universalists must act on the preferential option for life. We must take the lead by choosing life, by being "good neighbors," an option not available to everyone:

> ....many humans cannot afford to be good neighbors. Over two billion people rely on wood for household fuel, for example, and the supply for seventy percent of them is insecure. Their hope is that they can get three to four sticks a day in order to have minimum fuel for cooking or heating....Others, I among them, have greater choice in the matter. As members of dominant social classes we have the luxury to change our behavior patterns and to work toward more just social orders so that others, too, can live more lightly on the earth. We also have the responsibility to relinquish much of our power and privilege . *(McDaniel 1990, 230)*

Our responsibility is clear. It means choosing a preferential option for the poor by choosing balance and limits, the essence of the Cosmos; it means siding with life so that all people can live unoppressed and live with the benefits of humanization. The preferential option for life is the way of Cosmocentric Liberation Theology.

The Reign of God

The Reign of God or the Beloved Community is a time when people will be equal as written about by de Gruchy: their "hunger and their thirst for righteousness and social justice" will be satisfied (de Gruchy, 136). The Reign is not an existing order. The coming of the Reign will have a new point of departure. Bonino explains:

> The true question is not "What degree of justice (liberation of the poor) is compatible with the maintenance of the existing order?" but *"What kind of order, which order is compatible with the exercise of justice (the right of the poor)?"*
> Here alone do we find an adequate point of departure for the theological determination of priorities. The fixed point is "justice, the right of the poor." This is the theological premise from which we cannot depart. The variable to be explored has to do with the conditions and possibilities of an order that can best bring that right to fulfillment. *(Bonino, 86)*

The current order is an anthropocentric one in which God is separate from the cosmos. In this dualistic perspective, justice, as Bonino suggests, cannot be built without encouraging dehumanization. Instead, a new order compatible with justice must be created. The place to begin is with an ecocentric or Cosmocentric Theology of Liberation, where the needs of all living things are kept in balance, where all of life is divine. This, then, will be the Reign of God.

The Reign is a utopian concept (see pages 11-12). Block suggests (Bonino, 90-91) it serves an important role in an Ecocentric Liberation Theology. There is also a striking degree of similarity between its role and that of free or heuristic theology. Like free theology, it is a protest against the current anthropocentric order, that is, the theo-political status quo. Second, it challenges existing notions and introduces unthought-of possibilities. And third: "....it demands the immediate realization of such a new society, without delay and intermediate states, thus rejecting the 'tyranny of reality' which the dominant ideologies try to impose" (Bonino, 91).

As a utopian ideal, the Reign is a catalyst for change. But it isn't completely in the future since we see ecocentric breakthroughs whenever and wherever the oppressed reclaim balance, equality, and justice for the living. At these points, small as they may be, we catch a glimpse of the potential for humankind and all of life.

The Reign includes an understanding of the new order's needs, an understanding of what must happen to bring about a new order. The new order will blend consciousness and action, awareness and commitment, and achieve justice through balancing all of life's needs with the Cosmic order; there will be balance that will initiate humanization and Cosmocentric stability. This is more difficult than it sounds: perceiving the need for change, *convincing people* to share their power in order to achieve balance and limits, will not come easily. The struggle for awareness will come slowly. Ellis explains:

> Norman Podhoretz, a leading Jewish neoconservative, woke up one morning and realized it was better to be rich than poor, better to be powerful than weak. In some ways this has been a collective wakening rather than an individual's inspiration. Few would argue with his general theme unless an alternative was presented: that it is better for all to have access to the goods of life and be empowered to participate equally in the decision-making process in society. However, to reach this goal is to understand how affluence is created and how in its creation others are denied. As defined in our society, power demands the weakness of others and feeds on that weakness. *(Ellis 1987, 117)*

It is this kind of assessment that prompted Dorothy Soelle to return to the Exodus story. She suggests that if the oppressed are the Hebrews, then we (of the North Atlantic community) are the Egyptians, and if not the Egyptians then we have accommodated to an Egyptian-like lifestyle. Soelle says:

> The real exile of Christians in the First World is that we have learned to endure it. We have adjusted ourselves so much to Egypt that we feel at home. We have adopted the basic beliefs of the Egyptians....We have learned to endure the exile so well that we no longer see ourselves as exile people - as strangers in a strange land. Quite the contrary, we attempt to Egyptianize the whole world.... We see no need for liberation. *(Bayer 1986, 19)*

The tensions are clear: On the one hand is a comfortable, largely anthropocentric (and for those of the First World, largely ethnocentric) lifestyle that supports an imbalance of life-sustaining and life-nurturing resources that results in dehumanization and oppression of life in all nations; on the other hand are Cosmocentric breakthroughs (of the Reign) that depict an oppressive-free world of justice where balance and limits ensure freedom for life, yet members of the First World must learn to share power in order that others may live without the fear of injustice. The tensions *should* be obvious. What can be done? Marc Ellis writes:

> The question, it seems, is not how to go beyond the tension but how to move constructively within it. The choice to be with and for the empire in this struggle seems on the face of it, to be safer and less complex: to choose to move with those who seek community is to promote a configuration that may change....the perception of the world and of ourselves. By placing ourselves in the struggle for justice, we....may discover the other side of our own history. *(Ellis 1987, 75-76)*

The other side is an ecocentric side. The risk of free theology is the risk of broadening our view and becoming aware of Reign breakthroughs. Utopian in its vision, the Reign represents our struggle to achieve fullness in life, a struggle that by its very nature must be tension filled.

The Language of Liberation Theology

In the early stages of writing *A Reason For Hope*, I had a one meeting relationship with a seminary professor who displayed little faith or hope in the development of a Unitarian Universalist Theology of Liberation. Our meeting was marred by his verbal and nonverbal signs of disbelief, antagonism, and sarcasm for a Unitarian Universalist entering the arena of liberation theology. In short, he questioned if it could be done.

I was confused and offended by his insensitivity and intolerance for a faith tradition, perspective, and cultural experience different from his. This episode represents the kind of academic parochialism that McFague cites as a reason for the shortcomings of liberation theology (McFague 1991, 13). The exchange (or lack of it) also reflects the difficulty that most Unitarian Universalists have, and what individuals like this professor are aware of and sensitive to: an inability or refusal to understand and to use the language of liberation theology. Refusing to use the language of liberation theology could be a result of ignorance, confusion, or an intolerance for traditional Christian vocabulary. Whatever the reason, there has been no strong Unitarian Universalist voice in liberation theology circles, a silence that could be interpreted as a lack of interest or commitment from Unitarian Universalists.

While the language of an ecocentric or Cosmocentric Liberation Theology has many outstanding features to it and avoids the theological language offensive to some, this isn't the only direction to move: the openendedness of free theology encourages us to pursue other paths. What I am suggesting is that there is an urgent need for Unitarian Universalists to translate personal, community, and Association beliefs (like the *Principles and Purposes*) into the language of liberation theology in order to make clear our support for the liberation of life. It is my hope that the explorations in this chapter have contributed to clarifying and supporting further work toward awareness and action.

Chapter Four

CONCLUSION:
A REASON FOR HOPE

CONCLUSION:
A REASON FOR HOPE

*Do we believe that simply to think
about an issue is the same as to
live in a way which exemplifies
our concern for the issue?*

-- Thandeka

The creation of a Unitarian Universalist Theology of Liberation demands a reflection of Unitarian Universalism's rich history and contemporary faith. The selection, synthesis, and reformation of liberation language in the liberal faith tradition will nurture and promote an awareness that is important to formulating a new theological paradigm. One way of accomplishing this is simply to plunge into the books, articles, and other available presentations and experiences that focus on liberation themes. "Liberation Theology for Religious Liberals: A Curriculum For the Church" is designed with that purpose in mind (see Appendix 1). The curriculum can be used by one person though enriched by small and large group discussions. Educational in nature and exploratory in style, the curriculum is a catalyst for critiquing North Atlantic social and theological assumptions and introducing class members to liberation themes.

The field of liberation theology is an expanding one, not simply of passing interest. I heard a seminary professor comment to a class that the first millennium of theology was written by the East; the second by the West. The third millennium of theology will be shaped by the South, "from below," that is, it will be shaped by liberation theology. Awareness of the growing liberation movement has great significance.

Awareness is important, but the process of developing a contextualized liberation theology cannot stop there. In order for liberation theology to retain its dialectical charac-

61

ter, awareness must give impetus to action. Lawrence Swaim suggests that the most effective way for this to occur is based on a Latin American approach: "I suggest small discussion groups similar in many ways to the *communidad de base* (that is, base community) developed by Catholic followers of Liberation Theology in Latin America" (Swaim 1988, see Appendix 4). He goes on to explain:

> A small group of people - seven or eight, say - would meet regularly to talk about issues of social justice....Because this would evolve in a North American context, groups would reflect many characteristics of the group therapy session and the self-help group....When applied to liberal religion in North America, in other words, the *communidad de base* would be neither a self-help group, a religious group, but a new combination of all three....It would be a decision by politically-involved people to organize themselves in a particular church, but stressing emotional support in a totally new way - which would make it much different in tone than the secular Left. A common thread in these groups would be a willingness to examine power relationships at all levels - and even to translate that into personal or collective projects that could proceed at the group's (or individual's) own pace. *(Swaim, 118)*

Swaim has a specific intent in mind with the creation of these church-based communities, but his is not the only approach. Two others are available; both, like Swaim's, will create opportunities for awareness, exploration, and sharing at many levels while allowing for the freedom of design.

First, Scott Peck discusses the context and meaning of community. He also describes the "stages of community-making" (Peck 1987, 86), an interesting, enlightening and easy-to-read guide for group building. A second model to be considered is "AACTAC: A Human Process for Gathering Data and Making Decisions" (Fink, see Appendix 2). The ACCTAC model is based on six integrated steps: awareness, acceptance, caring for, trusting in, affirming, and celebration. With close attention to these critical steps, any individual or group can experience meaningful decision-making and community-building.

Why the importance of this community-building? Because of the urgent need for interdependency and wholism: "....to refuse to take responsibility for nurturing, loving, and befriending the body and all its parts" is sin, according to McFague (McFague 1990, 217). She is not alone; Herzog speaks of sin in terms of power: "In its root, sin is usurpation - the human attempt to wrest power from God, personally to play God with our neighbor" (Herzog 1988, 21).

Why the need for "liberation groups," or for that matter a Unitarian Universalist Theology of Liberation? Because the third millennium will not support a religious faith and church built on the premise of modern individualism (as suggested by Bellah, McFague, and others) - as Unitarian Universalism is (as suggested most strongly by Wright). The tenets of the Unitarian Universalist tradition as expressed and encouraged by liberal faith must be abandoned for a pluralism that is eclectic in theology (as *can* be found in our churches) and in people (which is rare in our churches). Bayer pieces together many of the loose threads and captures some of the concerns:

> I am convinced with the church, at least the church as we middle-class, mainline, First World people experience it ....Why is it we seek so few working class people in our worship services or in other phases in our parish programs? Why is there such a sense of loneliness and boredom pervading our congregations and our extra congregational religious institutions? Why do so many of us find it necessary to live safe, prophylactic, adventureless lives? *(Bayer, 153)*

Community-building or group-building, as in liberation theology, offers a lifeline of institutional hope, pulling us out of a darkened, murky, and lifeless sea of modern individualism. It is appropriate, then, to raise a question implicit to this work, but never asked. What is the role of the church? Thandeka probes further:

> Do we go to church in order to look into the darkness of

> our souls and face the hard truths of our existence? Do
> we go to church to gain the courage and community we
> need in order for us to make the courageous leap of faith
> into the terrifying truths of our lives? Do we go to
> church to stand over-against ourselves and pull our-
> selves into the hard truths of our existence? *(Thandeka,
> 46)*

To answer these questions, we leave the institutional
emphasis of this work and enter the individual one. The
struggle referred to by Thandeka is at the essence of theodicy, a critical issue in liberation theology. Ellis also writes
about the "darkness of our souls and the hard truths of our
existence" as it might be experienced in a community with
pluralistic integrity. He says: "Could it be that we are not
alone in the night but are joined by sisters and brothers in
a new continuity of struggle and affirmation?" (Ellis 1987,
80) Here, according to Ellis, is where solidarity will be
achieved. Solidarity is "....the movement of the heart,
mind, and body toward those who are suffering" (Ellis, 93).
Solidarity is the process that will bring both institutions
and individuals out of the night of loneliness (as reflected
in modern individualism) and into the light of relationship
(as reflected of pluralism). He concludes:

> Though often seen as a movement outward toward oth-
> ers, as something added to a fulfilled life, solidarity actu-
> ally is a journey to ourselves as well. It is an attempt to
> reclaim our humanity, bruised and alienated when our
> lives are built on the exploitation of others. This is true
> of a solidarity with our own community as well, for the
> journey toward others is at the same time a journey to-
> ward the foundation of one's own community. One can
> posit the opposite: a person or community that refuses
> solidarity ultimately refuses itself. *(Ellis, 93)*

Bayer, from a different perspective, reaches a conclusion not unlike the one suggested by Ellis:

> Liberation theology offers a way out of the grimness of
> our spiritual ennui and our prophylactic lifestyles. The
> path from boredom to freedom runs through the high-

land of passion. If we are to be set free from our captivity to the grayness, which marks the religious climate of our congregations, it will be as we recover the bundle of emotions, feelings and energies called passion. The freedom and adventure *passion* brings may enable us to discover the robust life. *(Bayer, 153)*

Solidarity and passion - in institutions and individuals - these are the essence of a Unitarian Universalist Theology of Liberation. So much is at stake. The risks are many and the rewards will be immeasurable.

LIBERATION THEOLOGY FOR RELIGIOUS LIBERALS

A Curriculum For the Church

LIBERATION THEOLOGY
FOR RELIGIOUS LIBERALS

One might say that theology undergoes transformation when the members of a community feel compromised; creativity and innovation emerge as persons encounter contradictions in life about which they cannot be silent.

-- Paul G. King

A Reason For Hope: Liberation Theology Confronts A Liberal Faith can be explored with a small group. While the curriculum is ideal for Unitarian Universalists, it can, of course, be adapted to meet the needs of any group of religious liberals who wish to respond to the challenge posed by Latin American Liberation Theology. The overall aim of this curriculum is to encourage participants to become politically and pastorally conscious of their involvement in the church and the larger community as an expression of their understanding of liberation theology.

In addition, through a shared, small group experience, this curriculum creates an opportunity for group members to become a model of the shift from (North Atlantic) individual consciousness to (Emerging World) group awareness. The curriculum can be used from 5 to 8 weeks (included here is an 8 week curriculum), two hours for each session depending on the needs of the group. Anything less than 5 weeks will not cover the material and will probably fall short of meeting the group's expectations. The church newsletter, Sunday morning announcements, the order of service bulletin, personal invitation and word of mouth can all be used to encourage class registration. As for group size, I recommend nothing larger than 20.

The aims of the curriculum are:

1. To stimulate and encourage an awareness and understanding of Latin American Liberation Theology - its context and theo-ethical sources and themes.

2. To explore, interpret and adapt religious liberal theo-ethical ideas and sources with liberation theology themes which could lead to a Unitarian Universalist Liberation Theology.

3. To examine and reflect on the personal and institutional impact of liberation themes.

4. To explore and encourage the personal integration and institutional impact of liberation themes.

5. To promote and nurture group support and solidarity.

Resources for the class include (again, these should be adapted to meet your own needs though it is important to keep the same themes):

James Luther Adams' "Five Smooth Stones of Liberalism" as found in *On Being Human Religiously* (Boston: Beacon Press, 1976).

Jason Berry's "A Theology for El Savador" as found in *The Washington Post*, November 26, 1989. For this resource, it might be best to use any current article on Latin America which specifically talks about Liberation Theology. See your local library's reference librarian.

Phillip Berryman's *Liberation Theology: The Essential Facts About the Revolutionary Movement in Latin America and Beyond* (New York: Pantheon Books, 1987). This text or a similar one is recommended for ongoing reading throughout the course.

Robert Evans' "Prophet or Provocateur?" found in *Human Rights* (Orbis Books: Maryknoll).

Bill Moyers, *"God and Politics: A Kingdom Divided,"* 90 minute videotape, 1989.

Lawrence Swaim's unpublished essay "The Case for a Unitarian Universalist Left" as found in Appendix 4.

The UUA's *Principles and Purposes*, Appendix 3.

"Theology and Activism," a talk given by William R. Jones at the 1989 General Assembly in New Haven, CT, moderated by Judith Meyers, and available from the UUA Distribution Center, 25 Beacon Street, Boston, MA 02108.

SESSION I

Goals

1. *Establish class calendar and expectations.*

2. *Create an opportunity for each group member to know at least one other member.*

3. *Clarify any questions regarding the class.*

4. *Begin discussion of Unitarian Universalism.*

Class

Make sure everyone fills out and wears a name tag - never assume that everyone knows everyone else. It's advisable to wear name tags for the first several sessions, if not for the whole course.

After going through the class expectations and answering questions, move into an exercise that will allow each member to become acquainted with at least one other member. For example, pair the group up and have each person "interview" their "mate" for 5 minutes with the intention of introducing that person to the group. Depending on the size of the group, this exercise and the introductions will take at least half the class time. It is critical to the interaction of the class that members feel comfortable in the group. Don't underestimate the importance of an "icebreaking" exercise of this sort. Also make sure to always take a break about halfway through the session.

With the remaining time of this session, the focus will be on faith and authority, that is, as Unitarian Universalists, where do we get our authority? What is the basis of authority for building our faith? In order to promote discussion, present the following paradigm:

SOURCES OF AUTHORITY	
FAITH TRADITION	**SOURCE OF AUTHORITY**
Catholicism	the structure (hierarchy)
Protestantism	the Gospels
Judaism	tradition
Unitarian Universalism	human experiemce

These are not exclusive categories, but each faith tradition tends to center on or filter through one form of authority, and only then does it bring into play the others (which also are important). For example, the primary focus for Unitarian Universalism is human experience. This isn't to say that structure, the Gospels and tradition aren't important, but it's not the primary one. This is to say that only through human experience are other sources of authority evaluated.

It is best to go through each of the faith traditions and sources of authority one by one, encouraging discussion about each.

Assignment

For Session II, read Adams' "Five Smooth Stones of Liberalism."

SESSION II

Goals

1. *To continue a discussion of the strengths and weaknesses of our own faith system and tradition.*

2. *To continue building group solidarity.*

Class

Start the class by asking for questions that might have carried over from the last week or provide any further clarification on the paradigm that was presented. Continuing on with the paradigm, it highlights that theology is a reflection on faith which reveals one's source of authority. Given this understanding, what is it then that characterizes and distinguishes Unitarian Universalist theology? That is, what sets it apart as liberal religion? In order to promote discussion on this, suggest these possible ways of looking at faith:

VISION is that aspect of faith which comprises a person's attitude about living. The questions that emerge from vision include: What do I believe about living? What is my attitude about living? What is my ultimate view or goal?

ACTION is an aspect of faith which forms the paradigm or scheme by which a person's reality works? Is there a definable system or scheme? What is the character by which the world is ordered?

WORLD VIEW is that part of faith that provides a larger context, a frame of mind: What do I believe about humankind in the world? What is my stance toward this?

Am I hopeful or hopeless?

INDIVIDUALISM is that part of faith which assigns meaning to the role, function or definition of a person. Questions might be: What is the role of individuals?, especially as we relate to one another. What is the character of this relation?

INSTITUTIONALISM is that aspect of faith which speaks about the role and meaning of groups in society. The questions that emerge here could include: What is the nature (and purpose) of institutions? What kind of institutions are we striving for?

As these elements of faith are framed in a Unitarian Universalist context, note how each one passes through the authority source of human experience (post the "Sources of Authority" grid). How might these five aspects be framed in the language of Unitarian Universalism? Here's your opportunity to present your own view. You could spell it out this way:

VISION: UUism asserts that heaven and hell are in this life, on earth, not something in the afterlife.

ACTION: UUism affirms that life is a process (in process). Continual movement is the essence of life and the universe.

WORLD VIEW: UUism asserts that humankind is essentially good.

INDIVIDUALISM: UUism celebrates the differences that people use to order their lives.

INSTITUTIONS: UUism suggests that social institutions and religious ones are not easily separated, but that the sacred and secular are often interdependent.

Place this statement of faith on a piece of newsprint, beginning on the left side with the "Element of Faith" (vision, action, world view, etc.) and moving to the right, leaving space for other column entries: one for Adams and then others. It should look something like this:

EXPRESSIONS OF FAITH		
ELEMENTS OF FAITH	**UUISM**	**ADAMS**
Vision	Heaven & Hell Now	
Action	Process	
World View	Human Good	
Indivlism.	Autonomy/ Pluralism	
Institutlism.	Social - Rel. Interdep.	

At this point, it will be time to take up the Adams essay. Following are quotes that might help guide the class toward forming an interpretation of the essay:

VISION: "...religious liberalism affirms the moral obligation to direct one's efforts toward the establishment of a just and loving community." (16)

ACTION: "Religious liberalism depends first on the principle that 'revelation' is continuous. Meaning has not been finally captured. Nothing is complete, and thus nothing is exempt from criticism. Liberalism itself, as an actuality, is patient of this limitation. At best, our symbols of communication are only referents and do not capsule reality. Events of word, deed and nature are not sealed. They point always beyond themselves. Not only is significant novelty both possible and manifest, but also significance is itself inchoate and subject to inner tensions of peril and opportunity." (12)

WORLD VIEW: "....liberalism holds that resources (divine and human) that are available for the achievement of meaningful change justify an attitude of ultimate optimism." (19)

INDIVIDUALISM: "Now, anything that exists effectively in history must have form. And the creation of a form requires power. It requires not only the power of thought, but community requires the organization of power. Through the organizations of power, liberated persons tie into history...." (18)

INSTITUTIONALISM: "....all relations between persons ought ideally to rest on mutual, free consent and not on coercion....the liberal's belief that the method of free inquiry is best for the preservation of human dignity." (14-15)

Following a discussion of these five elements of faith and then filling in the grid, it may look like this:

EXPRESSIONS OF FAITH		
ELEMENTS OF FAITH	**UUISM**	**ADAMS**
Vision	Heaven & Hell Now	Just/Loving Community
Action	Process	Revelation
World View	Human Good	Ultimate Optimism
Indivlism.	Autonomy/ Pluralism	Power & Organizn.
Institutlism.	Social - Rel. Interdep.	Freedom of Assoc. & Inquiry

This will conclude Session II.

Assignment

For Session III, begin reading Berryman's *Liberation Theology*.

SESSION III

Goals

1. *To continue discussion of Unitarian Universalist elements of faith.*

2. *To begin drawing the relationship between Unitarian Universalist faith and liberation theology.*

3. *To continue developing group cohesiveness.*

Class

Start the class with any follow up from the previous week. Then show the William Jones videotape "Theology and Activism." Following the presentation, refer back to the "Expressions of Faith" paradigm, create a new column to the right of "Adams" and label it "Jones." Work with the class toward completing the grid under "Jones." The following ideas and suggestions from Jones might help in directing the discussion:

VISION: "I am not hopeless, but not hopeful. Human beings will determine the future, the future is not planned."

ACTION: Oppression is due to a "gross imbalance of power which one group uses to exploit another." Jones believes in power-sharing.

WORLD VIEW: "There is no neutral theology: our theologies are either going to be of and for the oppressor, or they are going to be of and for the oppressed." There's no neutral ground.

INDIVIDUALISM: "Oppression operates primarily on inequality, so..." Jones believes in power-sharing or co-equality to be achieved through power-sharing.

INSTITUTIONALISM: Jones' analysis of society and oppression is institutional since institutions form the basis
of power.

With this, the class paradigm might look like this:

EXPRESSIONS OF FAITH

ELEMENTS OF FAITH	UUISM	ADAMS	JONES
Vision	Heaven & Hell Now	Just/Loving Community	Not Hopeful Not Hopeless
Action	Process	Revelation	Power Share
World View	Human Good	Ultimate Optimism	No Neutrality
Indivlism.	Autonomy/ Pluralism	Power & Organizn.	Social - Econ. & Pol. =
Institutlism.	Social - Rel. Interdep.	Freedom of Assoc. & Inquiry	Inst. & Group Inquiry

It will be necessary to end at this point.

Assignment

For the next session, come prepared to discuss the
Swaim essay, "The Case for a Unitarian Universalist Left."

SESSION IV

Goals

1. *To continue discussion of Unitarian Universalist elements of faith.*

2. *To continue drawing the relationship between Unitarian Universalist faith and liberation theology.*

3. *To continue developing group cohesiveness.*

Class

Consider the Swaim essay, using the "Expressions" paradigm. This time, add "Swaim" as a new column to be filled out. If you wish, use the following quotes as a guide for your discussion.

VISION: "Because they cannot motivate people to make difficult choices, because they do not understand the systemic nature of evil, because they suffer from institutional cowardice and timidity, both political and religious liberalism have become part of the problem rather than part of the solution. Both forms of liberalism must be transcended. Political liberalism must become some form of democratic socialism; liberalism must become social religion. (126)

ACTION: "UUs don't like to think so, but evil exists. So does sin. It is evil when parents abuse their children. It is sinful when the state pays people to rape and murder dissenters. We know these things not because they violate the scriptures of a holy book, but because they violate life. Evil is aggression, expressed usually as violence and exploitation, accompanied by the deceit that makes both possible. And it is *culturally transmitted*

81

through institutions, beginning with the family and ending with the armed state. (115)

WORLD VIEW: *"The real spiritual unrest of our time emanates from problems that can be addressed and changed only through cooperative political action.* (119)

INDIVIDUALISM: "Discussion of personal problems might be encouraged, depending on the wishes of the group. The overeater, the potential child abuser, the widow reentering the job market, the gay or lesbian person struggling with lifestyle issues - all would receive support from the group. But since these groups would be organized for a political purpose, participants would try to relate these personal issues to larger issues of institutional power, and to give each other support precisely to change the system. When applied to liberal religion in North America, in other words, the *communidad de base* would be a new combination of all three (styles of groups). It would acknowledge that in America the problem is not only institutional, but is also in the way we think and feel about power, and about making money. (118)

INSTITUTIONALISM: "I suggest small discussion groups similar in many ways to the *communidad de base* developed in Latin America....I would prefer to see them in the basements of churches." (118)

Having discussed the Swaim essay, the "Expressions of Faith" grid might now look like this:

▶

EXPRESSIONS OF FAITH				
ELEMENTS OF FAITH	**UUISM**	**ADAMS**	**JONES**	**SWAIM**
Vision	Heaven & Hell Now	Just/Loving Community	Not Hopeful Not Hopeless	Social Religion
Action	Process	Revelation	Power Share	Attack Inst. Evil
World View	Human Good	Ultimate Optimism	No Neutrality	Must Act
Indivlism.	Autonomy/ Pluralism	Power & Organizn.	Social - Econ. & Pol. =	Religion is Political & Healing
Institutlism.	Social - Rel. Interdep.	Freedom of Assoc. & Inquiry	Inst. & Group Inquiry	Liberation Groups Oriented

Allow for discussion as time permits.

Assignment

For Session V, come having read the Berry article "A Theology for El Salvador."

SESSION V

Goals

1. *To continue building the cohesiveness of the group.*

2. *To beginning looking at Latin American Liberation Theology.*

Class

Begin this class by asking for questions or clarifying statements regarding the material covered in Session IV.

Make sure everyone has read the Berry article. Give people the opportunity to go back over it, but this time, using pen or pencil, highlight what they believe are the main themes discussed by him, i.e., the main points about Liberation Theology. When this is done, break the class up into small groups - four in a group would be good. Their assignment is to compile a list of the liberation themes presented by Berry and to be ready to share their findings with the class. Allow 30 minutes for this exercise.

After returning, go from group to group, writing down their ideas, recording no two similar items. Take a break after this exercise.

Upon returning, watch the Moyers tape, "God and Politics: A Kingdom Divided." This will conclude Session V.

Assignment

For next week, complete the Berryman book and bring in a list of the themes he develops (similar in the way that was done with the Berry article). Also come prepared to discuss the Moyers videotape as it relates to the "Expressions of Faith" grid.

SESSION VI

Goals

1. *To become familiar with some of the themes in Latin American Liberation Theology.*

2. *To continue building on group cohesiveness.*

Class

Begin the class with questions and clarifications since Session V covered a great deal of material. Make sure that the newsprint with the themes is posted. Discuss the Moyers videotape looking for additional themes or ones that would support those developed in the Berry article. Also, urge the class to reflect on the Berryman book and what themes he develops.

Following are themes developed by Berryman which fit into the "Expressions of Faith" grid. You can use these or others highlighted by the class to fill out the grid.

VISION: "The kingdom (reign) is a situation in which we can live together as brothers and sisters. As such it is a utopia." (158)

ACTION: "....a utopia that impels people to work here and now for 'partial realizations' of that kingdom. Thus, Nicaraguan Christians who are committed to the revolution do not believe that - or any form of organization in society - will be the kingdom. Nevertheless, they believe that it does indeed offer the possibility of a more real kind of solidarity among people and is thereby a modest but real 'approximation' of the kingdom." (158)

WORLD VIEW: "....the starting point to which it continually returns is this ongoing dialogue with the poor. "(42) "Poverty has three interrelated meanings: dehumanizing lack of material goods, openness to God, commitment in solidarity." (32) "Speaking of poverty, the bishops reaffirmed Medellin's 'clear and prophetic option expressing preference for, and solidarity with, the poor.' They then stated, 'We affirm the need for a conversion on the part of the whole Church to a preferential option for the poor, an option aimed at their integral liberation.'" (43-44)

INDIVIDUALISM: "Traditionally, local community leaders have tended to copy the existing models of the dominant society, by themselves being petty dictators or at most demagogic populists. By sharing leadership widely and seeking to act by consensus, base communities have given many people a sense of a grass-roots kind of democratic process. That experience in turn has made them more critical existing political procedures." (74)

INSTITUTIONALISM: "The social and political impact of base communities may be viewed in terms of (1) initial consciousness-raising, (2) their vision of life and motivation for involvement, (3) the sense of community and mutual aid and support they generate, (4) the experience of grass-roots democracy, (5) the direct actions they engage in, and (6) directly political effects. (72-73)

Now the paradigm, with the added column for liberation theology, might look something like this:

————————————————————▶

EXPRESSIONS OF FAITH					
ELEMENTS OF FAITH	UUISM	ADAMS	JONES	SWAIM	LIBERATION THEOLOGY
Vision	Heaven & Hell Now	Just/Loving Community	Not Hopeful Not Hopeless	Social Religion	Reign of God
Action	Process	Revelation	Power Share	Attack Inst. Evil	Reign Breakthroughs
World View	Human Good	Ultimate Optimism	No Neutrality	Must Act	Prefer. Option for Poor
Indivlism..	Autonomy/ Pluralism	Power & Organizn.	Social - Econ. & Pol. =	Religion is Political & Healing	Empowerment
Institutlism..	Social - Rel. Interdep.	Freedom of Assoc. & Inquiry	Inst. & Group Inquiry	Liberation Groups Oriented	Base Community

Pass out the UUA *Principles and Purposes* and take a little time to read them through. Then, have the members go back into their small groups to consider the difference between that UUA's *espoused expressions of faith* and the UUA's *faith in use*. This distinction was made in the Jones presentation. The best the small groups might be able to do is look at the expressions of faith in terms of their own church life, or perhaps in their own life. Allow 30 minutes for this exercise. When members return, ask for reports from each group to be transcribed onto newsprint under two columns: ESPOUSED FAITH and FAITH IN USE. Do as much as time permits.

Assignment

For next session, read the Evans article "Prophet or Provocateur?"

SESSION VII

Goals

1. *Continue building the solidarity of the group.*

2. *To reflect on the dynamic of liberation theology, Unitarian Universalism and individual responsibility.*

Class

Begin the session with an opportunity to finish up any-thing left from last session. Ask everyone to break into their small groups in order to discuss the Evans article. As they begin, each person should share their first reactions to the article (comfort, tension, identification, disassociation, anger, apathy). After everyone has had a chance to share their responses, as a group identify the characters and roles (as well as ideology if recognizable). Each group should record these on newsprint to share with the larger group. Allow 45 minutes for this exercise. Take a break as people are returning from their small groups.

During the second hour, each small group should take no more than 10 minutes to post their newsprint and share their findings. When each group has done this, look for the shared findings and discuss them.

Assignment

For Session VIII, group members should read Chapter III: "Toward a Unitarian Universalist Theology of Liberation."

SESSION VIII

Goals

1. *To discuss and develop a Unitarian Universalist Liberation Theology.*

2. *To discuss how this theology impacts on our individual lives and the life of our church.*

3. *To reach closure for the group.*

Class

Having heard from the group regarding material from the previous session, turn everyone's attention to the completed "Expressions" paradigm:

EXPRESSIONS OF FAITH					
ELEMENTS OF FAITH	UUISM	ADAMS	JONES	SWAIM	LIBERATION THEOLOGY
Vision	Heaven & Hell Now	Just/Loving Community	Not Hopeful Not Hopeless	Social Religion	Reign of God
Action	Process	Revelation	Power Share	Attack Inst. Evil	Reign Breakthroughs
World View	Human Good	Ultimate Optimism	No Neutrality	Must Act	Prefer. Option for Poor
Indivlism..	Autonomy/ Pluralism	Power & Organizn.	Social - Econ. & Pol. =	Religion is Political & Healing	Empowerment
Institutlism..	Social - Rel. Interdep.	Freedom of Assoc. & Inquiry	Inst. & Group Inquiry	Liberation Groups Oriented	Base Community

Now consider the possibility of a Unitarian Universalist Theology of Liberation. How could we translate from the last column, "Liberation Theology" into something that would be theologically meaningful for UUs. Chapter III suggests a cosmocentric approach. When placed into the grid it looks like this:

ELEMENTS OF FAITH	LIBERATION THEOLOGY	UU LIBERATION THEOLOGY
Vision	Reign of God	Cosmocentric Order
Action	Reign Breakthroughs	Cosmocentric Justice
World View	Prefer. Option for Poor	Balance & Limits
Individualism	Empowerment	Pluralism
Institutionalism	Base Community	Solidarity

The class might choose to list something all their own - this is to be encouraged. The hope is that discussion will be generated.

The rest of this final session is turned over to looking at what the group might be able to do for the church: continue meeting as a liberation group (as Swaim suggests), pursue further study, become a sub-group of the church's Social Justice Committee, plan a Sunday service. The options are many. And of course, this class might be the end. So be it.

AACTAC

Awareness - Acceptance - Caring - Trusting - Affirming - Celebrating

AACTAC

Awareness

Sensation/Desensitization

At any given moment we can be aware of innumerable sensations communicated to us from our external world (the environment) and from our own internal world (what goes on inside us). These are unlabelled and uncategorized.

Developmentally we are born into a world of sensation - the childhood experience of discovery, curiosity, delight, responsiveness, spontaneity, etc.

We cannot handle all the sensations so have learned to screen out or become desensitized to those that are painful, not important or relevant. Desensitization is an inevitable and at times a very useful part of growth, education, socialization, adapting, etc.

Sensation occurs along a continuum of awareness: unconscious....feelings. emotions. (labelled, categorized, clear figure)

Usefulness of desensitization allows us to eliminate distracting sensations and to identify and accomplish or reach our want, needs and goals.

Unaware, chronic, archaic desensitization produces dysfunction.

Desensitization develops from our use or underuse of a part of ourselves.

The more alive are our senses the greater the possibility for range, richness, clarity, focus, and identity of our awarenesses.

Development of sensing is a continuous over and over again process.

All resistences cause and require some desensitization - basic resistance

Things We Can Be Aware Of:

- Sensation (unlabelled)

- Emotions - patterns of organized sensations labelled and categorized

- Wants/needs

- Perceptions - organization of data - naming, representing

- External environment - acquire data which I choose and organize in percepts

- Thoughts, memories, images, fantasies, dreams, beliefs, values, plans, excuses, rationales, etc.

- Continues ongoing interaction between organism and environment

- Sensing may be active or passive - Awareness may be directed or undirected

Active/Directed		Passive/Undirected
seeing	vs.	looking
hearing	vs.	listening
feeling	vs.	touching
smelling	vs.	sniffing
tasting	vs.	sampling

Points Of Awareness:

- Awareness is self correcting, self regulating

- Awareness is figure/background process in which selection takes place.

- Need energizes the organism, energizes the perceptual field.

- Awareness of wants/needs leads to focused action and contact.

- Awareness - always in present, always changing - internal and external data.

- Awareness is the basis for knowing - with knowing comes possibility of choice, we can change ourselves and our environment.

- Purpose of awareness work - to get in touch with fixed gestalts, to see what we are doing, and how we are doing it so we can change by choices.

Pay Attention To:

- What is selected or avoided

- What is the characteristic pattern of awareness - e.g., to slide away from tension

- What is the balance between internal and external awareness

- What is the nature of the blocks and avoidance - e.g. that I focus too hard or intensively on one or two awarenesses and end up being confluent with them

Helper Needs Double Awareness

As a helper it is important to be aware of two aspects of awareness. To know what the awarenesses are in him/her and in the helpee so as to use as many awareness resources as possible to identify theme and be creative in developing experiments.

- What's going on in helper - e.g. awareness of his/her body sensation, breathing, thoughts that are totally unrelated to being with the other.

- Helpers thoughts, ideas, opinions, attitudes, memories that begin with him/her and are part of his/her perception of the other.

- Empathic being with the other - e.g. tuning into the other may result in our tuning ourselves so that we are resonating with them - example: tightening mouth when other does that, repressing breathing when other does that, etc.

Acceptance

Of What Is:

Awareness leads to change, and increased awareness leads to growth. Paradoxical Theory of Change, that change occurs when one becomes what he is, not what he tries to become what he is not.

Focus in on "what is," to increase the experience of "here and now" to take full ownership of one's present experience. Change occurs when a person becomes what he is or she is. Change grows out of the acceptance of "what is."

Emerging Figure:

Emerging from awareness is figure/ground. Selection of figure in the present moment versus attempted preselection of figure in the past for the present moment. Use of screen or bias to influence the upper most figure. Spontaneous selection of upper most figure carries the assumption that it may be possible to get at something within indirectly which cannot be contacted directly.

Obstacles to figure/ground process sometime called resistences.

- No figure emerges - "I am blank"
- Two competing figures emerge
- Multiple figure emerge which overwhelm
- Indistinct figures - not quite sure
- A clear figure emerges and no energy to work - exhausted

Of Theme:

Definition - a recurring unifying subject or idea - a motif

- thread around which awareness, energy, action evolves
- emergence of figure
- a myth, schema or screen through which we perceive our lives
- not good or bad, right or wrong. All themes are OK.

Purpose - theme is a unifyer/definer of what is in process
- organizes happenings into manageable units
- connects helper and client with an agreed upon focus
- focuses and raises energy of both client and helper
- gives boundaries to work that is possible
- begins to develop a direction for action

Seen In - stories people tell selves and others to make sense of experience
- transactions between people
- images, structure etc., which symbolize a process, style, intent, problem

PRESENTING STATEMENT - captures what people are interested in, energized by, and working on, as they interpret to others and also shows what they are having difficulty with - the unfinished business. The distilled essence of the client's concern.

Theme Development - a phenomenon or consequence of the helper-client interaction. Process includes:

- Helper's formulation of uppermost energized figure
- Assessment of client's energy regarding that figure
- Helper's statement of the figure and the direction to the client
- The client's response
- Modification (if needed) of theme so that both are engaged by it

RAISES ENERGY - it is in effect where the energy is located and/or where the energy is blocked.

LOSES ENERGY - If theme is foisted upon client, he/she will resist and energy will evaporate.

GIVES DIRECTION - Indicates where and/or how we stop ourselves - the direction to be taken.

ROLE CHANGE - Stating the theme and getting agreement marks the transition of the helper from attending and tracking the client's process through awareness to the taking of a more active part by beginning to generate a new experience.

CREATIVITY - A creative projection - to know and own something in yourself and to identify that something in another, to lovingly support another with respect and genuineness. Theme gives us a road map so we can know at all times a beginning, a middle and an end.

Caring

Taking Charge:

Mobilization - organizing for action
- reviewing awareness
- identifying figure
- paraphrasing theme

Resistances - a natural part of the self regulatory process of the person.
- Resistance exists for the safety and survival of the person, family, etc.
- Resistance allows choices.
- Resistance regulates degrees of tension.
- Resistance protects from being overwhelmed.
- Some form of resistance, some form of avoidance is at the heart of all emotional malfunctioning - habitual resistance.

Resistance is most often experienced as resisting something or someone outside the self, when in fact it is fundamentally resisting some part of the self (a disowned part or polarity). Therefore, resistance is the unwillingness to experience some part of the self - be it intellectual, physical, emotional, spiritual. That is, there is some injunction, some fear to be aware of, to activate and to interact from that aspect of the self.

The helper is not discouraged by resistances but rather

brings an attitude of curiosity, interest and support. Resistance is not "against us," it is the result of the person getting close to contacting - owning some part of themselves. This attitude requires of the helper a centeredness, a continuing process of awareness of self - me separate from us.

Chronic resistances were learned for a good reason and are now probably inappropriate.

Types of Resistances:
- Desensitization - shutting off senses, no awareness of or action toward the environment - boredom, blahs, inactivity
- Confluence - believing there is no difference between self and other, self and environment - clinging, hanging on behavior
- Introjection - identification with environment and denial of self - taking in, shoulding, pleasing, placating, depending, no questioning, fixation
- Retroflection - do to yourself what you like to do to others or do to yourself what you would like others to do to you
- Projection - environment experienced but is used as a screen to project inner feelings. It is disowning of experiencing
- Deflection

CARING FOR - the work of the helper is to bring the client's resistance in to awareness and engage it, activate it, interact with it. Allowing it to be fully what it is so it may be transformed from an unaware handicap into an energized supportive part of me.

EXPERIMENT - A tool that emerges out of the activity or passivity of a client over long periods of time and out of the helpers receptivity to their modes of being, client themes and the helpers active sharing in the process.

It is extremely important to pay attention to
- amount of tension and around what? If not enough one cannot produce, if too much there's the chance for im-

moblization
- what is the want - what organizes the energy
- what is/are the polarities
- where and/or what are the resistance points, points where the work has to be active
- use the client's own words - do not invent
- the closing action or words should be related to the opening statement or theme, completing a unity of work
- Work slowly, heighten resistance - if no resistance there is no growing

PARTNERSHIP - Remember you and your client are a system, neither of you can work alone. You must compliment and build on one another so that experiment may succeed and growth takes place.

CHANGE - The change process may be conceptualized as five steps:

1. Making aware what is;
2. Identifying the forces for change;
3. Identifying the forces for sameness (resistances);
4. Facilitate an interplay of these two forces;
5. Aware of what now is....

Trusting

Doing It

ASSUMPTION - Change, not sameness, is the basic nature of the universe. In the natural state there is constant change between the self and the world.

ARENA - Three important structures which are not static but rather are always in process. 1.) the organism, 2.) the environment, 3.) the boundary of the two. Interaction takes place at the boundary and it is at the boundary that you make contact, find change and the resistance to change.

COMMITMENT - We will do it. We will be active not passive. The client is the actor and the playwright. He/she is the potter and the clay, the designer and the designed with helper as co-director.

ACTION - putting into action the experiment never forgetting to continue to use your awarenesses for updating and modifying the experiment. Nothing is fixed, everything is subject to change so helper needs to constantly be aware of the first three steps acquiring new awarenesses, enlarging or adapting the theme, developing, modifying, reducing or changing the experiment. Happening in the here and now. Use of body in physical way to move, speak, emote, reach out and effect or impact our world.

CONTACT - actions with something in environment that satisfies need and taking it in; opening up boundaries to take in air, food, love, looks, taste, touch, sounds, smells.

Affirming

Appreciation

WE DID IT - affirmation of the piece of work we did, acknowledgement of the struggle and effort even if sense of satisfaction is not high. Resistances were confronted and a step was taken. Affirm both client and helper.

WITHDRAWL - moving away from contact either physically or shutting down the contact functions.

CENTERING - moving into center of self to assimilate experience; this is the process of change; restructuring.

ASSIMILATION - utilization of new material and the elimination of what is not useful (waste). Process of reintegration leads to a sense of completion.

BODY - equilibrium, inner stillness, contact with self, intense passive energy prior to moving on to a new set of sensations. Body shifts, let go.

AWARENESS - expand understanding of how something is happening now and what is happening now. Provide the ground out of which choice can emerge to close.

Celebrating

Worth

I can and will allow myself to affirm self and proclaim "I am of worth." I can and have experienced "self-worth" and know it is true.

UNITARIAN UNIVERSALIST ASSOCIATION PRINCIPLES and PURPOSES

UNITARIAN UNIVERSALIST ASSOCIATION PRINCIPLES and PURPOSES

We,
the member congregations of the
Unitarian Universalist Association
covenant to affirm and promote:

The inherent worth and dignity of every
person
Justice, equity, and compassion in human
relations
Acceptance of one another and encouragement
to spiritual growth in our congregations
A free and responsible search for truth
and meaning
The right of conscience and the use of the
democratic process within our congregations
and Society at large
The goal of world community with peace,
liberty, and justice for all
Respect for the interdependent web of all
existence of which we are a part.

The living tradition we share draws
from many sources:

Direct experience of that transcending
mystery and wonder, affirm in all
cultures, which moves us to a renewal
of spirit and an openness to the
forces that create and uphold life
Words and deeds of prophetic women
and men which challenge us to confront
powers and structures of evil
with justice, compassion, and the
transforming power of love

Wisdom from the worlds religions which

inspires us in our ethical and spiritual life
Jewish and Christian teachings which
   call us to to respond to God's love by
   loving our neighbors as ourselves
Humanist teachings which counsel us to
   heed the guidance of reason and the
   results of science, and warn us
   against idolatries of the mind and spirit.

Grateful for the religious pluralism
   which enriches and ennobles our faith,
   we are inspired to deepen our understanding
   and expand our vision. As free
   congregations we enter into this covenant,
   promising to one another our
   mutual trust and support.

The Unitarian Universalist Association
   shall devote its resources to and exercise
   its corporate powers for religious, educational,
   and humanitarian purposes. The
   primary purpose of the Association is to
   serve the needs of its member congregations,
   organize new congregations,
   extend and strengthen Unitarian
   Universalist institutions, and implement
   its principles.

Adopted as a Bylaw at the 1984 and 1985 General Assemblies.

THE CASE FOR
A UNITARIAN UNIVERSALIST LEFT

THE CASE FOR
A UNITARIAN UNIVERSALIST LEFT

by
Lawrence Swain

Rosario Godoy de Cuevas was a very special human being. She was a leader of the Guatemalan human rights movement. One bright spring morning in 1985 she set out on a shopping trip with her brother and her two-year-old son. She was found dead that evening. They had killed her brother and her baby, and they had suffocated her with a plastic bag tied around her neck. (Her dead baby's fingernails were missing, so they had probably tortured the infant to death in front of her - a favorite trick of the Guatemalan military.)

And of course they had raped her.

The purpose is not just to kill or maim the body, you see. The purpose is to kill that part of the personality people once called the soul. Whether they succeeded or not could depend - at least for you - on what you decide to think and feel about it. Because if you are an American citizen there is a very special connection between you and Rosario.

In 1954 the American CIA and the United Fruit Company overthrew a freely-elected government and installed a dictator. The US has been supporting increasingly violent dictatorships ever since. Since 1954 somewhere between 100,000 and a quarter of a million civilians have been slaughtered by the military. This enormous human tragedy was created in our name. Its motives were - and are - economic exploitation and political domination.

Of course, the part about economic exploitation doesn't often get into American newspapers. It's not something that is supposed to be part of political discourse in this country. It's easier to deal in abstractions and in vague geopolitical jargon. That way we don't have to see the person, we don't have to see the victim in life and in death - and in the hour before death.

That way we don't have to see the connection between ourselves and the victim.

Torture practiced by the state (either to extract information, or simply as a form of terrorism) is probably more common now than at any time in history. Systematic use of rape has become institutionalized in many Third World regimes, especially those supported by the United States. Selective assassination of people on the political Left and Center has been raised to the level of a fine art, again particularly in those dictatorships supported by the United States. And imprisonment of dissenters is such a reality in today's world that it is no longer even regarded as particularly noteworthy, except for propaganda purposes when dealing with an "official" enemy - that is, an enemy chosen by the state.

Accompanying these political realities is a horror unique to our age, the threat of nuclear annihilation. The fact is that in forty years neither the peace movement in the West nor Russia's small unofficial peace movement has had any real effect on the design, manufacture and deployment of nuclear weapons. In the meantime American capitalism is ever more disastrously predicated on ever-rising level of arms spending - Military Keynesianism, some economists call it - that makes settlement of the Cold War almost impossible.

Set in motion by these unprecedented events is a generalized crisis of culture. Americans increasingly see themselves as belonging to a new world upper class, to which American citizenship gives them automatic membership. A popular materialism has become the state religion of America, in which the marketplace has become not only highest reality, but the best and final test of virtue - the single standard by which most people live their lives. Permeating all of this is a malevolent belief-system in which people are encouraged to define their personalities not through cooperation, but competition - which all to often translates into some variety of patriarchal domination. One result is a breakdown of trust at every level of social interaction, including our most intimate relationships.

Political liberalism (which would have us believe that the crisis is happening because of certain bad ideas, and a few irrational decisions here and there) no longer satisfies. We sense the need for a more fundamental examination of power relationships in American life, especially economic ones - and the way money operates on the American mind.

What are good about economic power relationships in America? What are bad about them? How can people be empowered to correct them in a democratic way? Do our relationships with the Third World have to be based on exploitation? Why are our children taught that in economic matters competition is the highest good, and cooperation worthless?

Our most prophetic voices have told us repeatedly that social justice must become the new heart and soul of liberal religion. And we all sense that the next state in the struggle for social justice means looking closely at economic relationships. But to think about the possibility of structural flaws in American capitalism is to cross an invisible line that is drawn everywhere in our national life and thought, a line we have been conditioned all our lives not to cross. The message is simple: "If you criticize capitalism, you are a Communist, and the state will punish you." Of course this isn't true, but on some level we tend to buy it. And despite our easy talk of tolerance we are no more prepared than the average Southern Baptist to think or discuss dangerous thoughts, and perhaps less so. The result is a dangerous, guilt-ridden malaise about who we are and where we are going.

So while conservative Christian evangelicals have met the crisis with their twin saviors (Jesus being the personal savior and Reagan the political one), our denomination has become a school for various kinds of upper-middle-class dilettantism. Since it can be whatever anyone wants it to be, the inclination of most people is quite naturally to make it into something completely safe, in which nobody needs to make any real changes. This makes it especially attractive to educated people who are frightened by the crisis through which we are passing, but who don't particularly want to do anything about it. Thus the denomination is ideally suited to becoming a device for escaping - and denial. "Much that passes for a benign tolerance for the opinions of others," wrote John Morely, "is in truth only a pretentious form of being without settled opinions of our own, or any desire to settle them." Morely could easily have been writing about many of today's UUs.

Because we have neither creed nor strong voices, a sensibility has arisen in which it becomes a positive virtue to believe in nothing. Instead of strong beliefs to cherish and debate, we celebrate "process," a codeword for the unwillingness to make moral choices (which is also a form of nihilism). Or UUs try to be all things to all people, an adjunct to the human potential movement: pop psychology, pop Zen, pop feminism, pop meditation, you name it - all of which usually adds up not to enlightenment, but to pop religion at its most narcissistic. Beneath these fads and fashions (and only partially repressed by them) is the guilt we feel at being unwilling to really confront the great issues of the day, which in America almost always involve an unspoken but ever-present economic agenda. At its worst our denomination becomes a middlebrow inspirational service, offering watered-down Emersonian uplift to an increasingly alienated upper-middle-class, alluding vaguely to problems but seldom encouraging people to debate them openly.

That is not tolerance. That is spiritual laziness.

Religion should teach us to make commitments, and to discuss and renegotiate them regularly. Modern Unitarian Universalism cannot teach such negotiating skills because it does not teach commitment in the first place. Instead it teaches people not to take risks, not to come down on one side of an issue or the other. That is not freedom, but the very essence of moral irresponsibility. This cultural style, which shows signs of becoming the style of large sections of the American upper-middle-class, is little more than a highly intellectualized method for distancing (and alienating) oneself from everything in life that can deeply touch or disturb the human heart and mind.

Above all it becomes a way of repressing an awareness of pain - and of evil.

UUs don't like to think so, but evil exists. So does sin. It is evil when parents abuse their children. It is sinful when the state pays people to rape and murder dissenters. We know these things not because they violate the scriptures of a holy book, but because they violate life. Evil is aggression, expressed usually as violence and exploitation, accompanied by the deceit that makes both possible. Ands *it is culturally transmitted through institutions,* beginning with the family and ending with the armed state.

The conservative Christian evangelicals understand the existence of evil, understand the role it plays in peoples' lives. They have an answer. The answer is called substitutionary atonement - which means that Jesus will take responsibility not only for your sins, but also for forgiving you. And you are guaranteed eternal life.

There are not many people left in our denomination who believe in such atonement. So if we want to confront evil it becomes necessary to develop an analysis of how it operates in the present moment - in institutions, in power relationships, in belief-systems and in our personal lives. Many UUs don't like to do that. The whole subject of evil makes us nervous, and we particularly don't like to look at how it operates in economic arrangements. That's too close to home.

Yet when we examine evil in American life, we find that issues of power and profit usually play a major role. Even in the most intimate situations we find that the abuse of power is usually the problem. And since most of our most important personal values derive from those norms and incentives at work in public life, a political analysis of public evil become a necessity. But here is where the problem begins. *You cannot explore systemic or institutional evil in America without developing a critical attitude toward some aspects of American capitalism.* And that means going against a lifetime of ideological conditioning. Even to have such ideas - that capitalism is neither perfect nor automatically self-correcting - is to take a dizzying step outside the comfortable confines of mainstream liberalism into a terrain usually identified with the Left. And the Left - even the most democratic kind of Left - is territory that to the average UU (as to the average American) is not only relatively unknown, but genuinely frightening.

So rather than face the reality of evil we UUs hide in the vagaries of pop religion.

Even the most gifted satirist would have trouble coming up with a better example of pop religion (or rather, pop politics) than the current UU drive to declare churches nuclear-free zones. Some defenders of this program maintain that it is a kind of theatre, in which people are allowed to confront certain issues they would normally repress. I think it is just another form of denial. It will allow a lot of nice people to do something that means exactly nothing, and imagine that they have done something real. Perhaps that is the true function of our denomination in American culture, to create that kind of illusion. Perhaps that is the liberal equivalent of the evangelical conversion experience - a little theatre in the suburbs, and then everything goes on exactly as before.

In recent times the UU WORLD has carried a political statement by, and a biographical profile of, two of my denominational brethren who are also political conservatives. I strongly support this, since as a democratic socialist I support freedom for all points of view. This is not just a powerful tradition within democratic socialism, but also within our own denomination. The history of King's Chapel during the American Revolution, for example, presents us with an inspiring example of radicals seeking to separate conservatives from political and civil power while at the same time caring for them and protecting their rights as spiritual brothers and sisters. This includes supporting their right to free speech even while vehemently opposing their ideas.

But there is another political minority within our denomination that - like the conservatives - frequently feels oppressed or overlooked by political liberalism. I refer to those associated with the religious Left. A growing number of UUs have been influenced by Liberation Theology, and agree with its insistence that issues of institutional power and profit must be probed before spiritual liberation is possible. In the past the religious Left has been associated mainly with the Roman Catholic church (because that is where Liberation Theology originated) and with certain other denominations, and has usually defined its role as meaning that the politics of social justice are one very expression of religion, especially when this involves radical analysis and advocacy. Some Unitarian Universalists would argue that such analysis and advocacy is - particularly when accompanied by art and the search for a new personal morality - itself a form of religion, and an important religious option for the future.

It is a sad commentary on our denomination that the WORLD, our denominational publication, regularly avoids any mention of specifically Left advocacy or commitment - at least until very recently. This does not occur by accident. In fact, there is considerable anxiety in the leadership of the UUA about fund-raising, which in turn influences - sometimes subtly and sometimes not so subtly - the contents of the publication. I am not interested in stigmatizing particular individuals, nor should radicals respond to this form of institutional evil by demanding a limit to the freedoms of UU conservatives and liberals. But we should demand that the denomination understand the nature of this evil, and we should organize to change it. At the very least, the executive in charge of fundraising should have no editorial control, and if the WORLD is to be anything but the most insipid kind of happy-talk it should be managed by a nonprofit corporation completely separate from the leadership of the UUA. At present the Vice President for Communications and Development - the person who is in charge of fundraising - has editorial control over every word of copy that appears in the WORLD, and although this person's decisions can theoretically be appealed to the President of the UUA, a conservative tone is set at the outset. This has resulted in the rightward drift of the publication and an intolerable conflict of interest at the top levels of our denomination.

To protest such abuses I call for the creation of a UU Left, a new movement that can challenge not only American society but liberal religion itself. This would be not just a new set of ideas to discuss but would, as I envision it, involve new forms of worship. I suggest small discussion groups similar in many ways to the *comunidad de base* (that is, base community) developed by Catholic followers of Liberation Theology in Latin America.

A small group of people - seven or eight, say - would meet regularly to talk about issues of social justice. One person might speak briefly on an assigned topic; another might give a brief reading. Discussion would follow, going around the circle and allowing each person to speak in turn to prevent the more articulate members from dominating the discussion. These groups would not be organized from the top down, but would be organized at the grassroots by politically-minded UUs themselves. Although these groups could meet in peoples' homes, I would prefer to see them in the basements of the UU churches themselves - a visible reminder to the rest of the church that they are there to have dialogue with them, to share with them, to challenge them, and ultimately to offer them the refuge of community at that point that they are ready to explore those issues of power and vulnerability that most Americans are afraid to talk about.

Because this would evolve in a North American context, groups would reflect many characteristics of the group therapy session and self-help group (such as AA, ACA and related 12-step programs). Discussion of personal problems might be encouraged, depending on the wishes of the group. The overeater, the potential child abuser, the widow re-entering the job market, the gay or lesbian person struggling with lifestyle issues - all would receive support from the group. But since these groups would be organized for a political purpose , participants would try to relate these personal issues to larger issues of institutional power, and to give each other support precisely to change the system. When applied to liberal religion in North America, in other words, the *comunidad de base* would be neither a self-help group, a religious group, nor a political group, but a new combination of all three. It would acknowledge that in America the problem is not only institutional, but is also in the way we think and feel about power, and about the making of money. It would be a decision by politically-involved people to organize themselves in a particular church, but stressing emotional support in a totally new way - which would make it much different in tone than the secular Left. A common thread in these groups would be a willingness to examine power relationships at all levels - and eventually to translate that into personal or collective projects that could proceed at the group's (or the individual's) own pace.

This is an important point. Americans desperately seek peace of mind in a variety of ways, through lifestyle changes, through psychotherapy, through the human potential or growth movements, through the desperate pursuit of inappropriate amounts of power and money and material possessions, and through pop religion and pop politics. Our new movement would insist that these gambits are increasingly doomed to failure, not just because they are often superficial, but because they are attempts to resolve societal problems through individual actions. *The real spiritual unrest of our time emanates from problems that can be addressed and changed only through cooperative political action.* On the other hand, our movement would acknowledge that real social change should occur as a kind of dualism, with institutional change accompanied by spiritual change within the individual. The UU Left would try to address both - but it would be unequivocal in its insistence that the key redemptive act, at least in our time, is one of commitment to social justice.

It would also insist that only the individual can decide for herself or himself what form that commitment should take. I tend to favor specific projects, because of the well-known UU tendency to substitute talk for action. But it is also true that such a commitment for some people might mean simply a change in attitude toward power relationships, change which would seem relatively uneventful to most observers but which is actually profound, and which can positively affect many lives.

I would suggest but one rule. To prevent the subtle regimentation that educated people are sometimes capable of, members of a group might agree not to criticize the beliefs of another member directly, but only to discuss what that issue has meant to them. For UUs that is a hard spiritual discipline, but very, very effective in building true equality, and true community - which for these groups might mean not just new ideas, but also some new and difficult feelings. For this to work, people will need the unconditional freedom to share things without being attacked.

The groups would also offer a safe place to discuss precisely those things that "politically correct" people are never supposed to talk about. What about the white progressive who has had a bad experience with a particularly abrasive Black person, and who now experiences negative feelings towards all Blacks? What about the person who has had a violent discussion about Israel with a right-wing Zionist and now finds herself feeling defensive and angry around other Jews? What about the Black or Latina woman struggling to over come negative feelings toward white women? UUs - and liberals in general - spend an astonishing amount of time and energy pretending that they never have these kinds of thoughts and feelings, but that is absurd. Everybody has these kinds of thoughts and feelings if they are human, and they become a problem only when people are afraid to talk about them.

Harvey Cox and others have called for the creation of such groups (base communities, liberation groups or whatever they decide to call themselves) among the poor of North America. I support this call. At the same time, I think there is the possibility for something equally radical among affluent people. I would like to hear upper-middle-class types talking about how oppression affects *them* . I would like to hear such people talk about how it feels to have their tax dollars used to murder people in Latin America - how it feels to live comfortably in a country in which the Black underclass is being systematically impoverished. I think we might discover what George Orwell pointed out at the height of the British empire: that unjust systems produce tension and unhappiness not only among those who are exploited by them, but among those who are supposed to benefit from them.

Although no one contemplates a national organization at present, liberation groups as a *network* could try to project the concerns and special values of the religious Left within the Unitarian Universalist denomination. Those influenced by Liberation Theology usually use a Marxist (or neoMarxist) analysis combined with a specific religious commitment, and many people associated with the religious Left are either committed pacifists, or believe in intelligent use of civil disobedience. A few are Marxist-Leninists. Any Left grouping within the UU denomination would be a home for socialists, pacifists and other political radicals, but would also be anxious to extend a fraternal hand to those who believe strongly in sanctuary and opposition to the arms race. It would especially welcome those radicalized by the lesbian, gay, feminist, peace, labor and minority movements, and would always be open to those who are struggling economically, and are ready to look at the way capitalism affects their lives.

Nor should it simply accept the values of the religious Left as it exists now - it should seek to engage, challenge and add to them from the special perspective of Unitarian Universalism. I believe our economic analysis should avoid the dangerous millennialism of doctrinaire Marxism and adopt instead the best teachings of the democratic socialists, teachings which are in no way a rejection of the democratic method, but which on the contrary advocate that it be extended into economic and corporate affairs at all levels. I suggest that we be willing explore the religious and secular roots of the best forms of pacifism (and of civil disobedience), and to examine the psychological and economic roots of war. I especially encourage socialist-feminists to take an active part in organizing groups, and I believe that Blacks, Latinos and other people or color should also be encouraged to take leadership roles. I would like to see our liberation groups develop those forms of study, worship and political support that reflect our unique UU insistence on the democratic method, both internally and in our political projects. And certainly we should feel free to find our own way to a cooperative ethic that can be described in secular terms, rather than a religious ethos based on scriptural interpretations.

The liberation groups would challenge the existing UU churches, would recruit from them, and would in turn seek to recruit from outside the church, with the express purpose of interesting more people in Unitarian Universalism. But I am completely opposed to seeking consensus on the church level, because that would be unfair to those who disagree with us. (Because of the conservative drift of many UU churches, such consensus is no longer very likely anyway, and Left groups might find it easier to link up with those outside the church on certain issues.) On the other hand, the liberation groups should not be shy about what they are doing, and why. If a group is serious about offering sanctuary to a Latin refugee, for example, members of the church to which they belong should be given the chance to meet the refugee themselves. Such a dialogue with the Other should never be forced - but it is precisely the function of the UU Left to insist that the presence of the victim not be denied, to create the circumstances through which the story of that victim can be told, and to publicly explore the extend to which the US dollar paid for that victimization.

Make no mistake about it: liberation groups would definitely test the denomination's commitment to tolerance, and not just because sanctuary would be a major issue for the UU Left. Our Left would be politically inclusive. That is, we would never turn anyone away for exclusively political reasons, including Communists and conservatives. We are well aware that in this country the real crunch usually comes at that point that Communists become involved in anything, and we should make it absolutely clear that as long as they do not try to take over the network, there will be no litmus test for any particular group - including any Communists who happen to be UUs. (Or Trotskyists or other Marxist-Leninists, for that matter.) Democratic socialists believe in the same freedom as liberals, but we intend to do a better job of protecting them that the liberal have done.

Tolerance, or toleration, has historically implied that one was willing to stand up against intolerance from the state. In modern times this intolerance usually takes the form of political persecution. What will happen when the UU Left - and the UUA along with it - are redbaited by the hirelings of an intolerant state? Will the good burghers of the UU churches scurry for cover, or will they stand up for freedom of speech and association?

There is a crisis in both religious and political liberalism, a crisis which at bottom is about the same thing - the problem of institutional evil. This crisis has been evolving, in one way or another, since the late 19th century.

In other industrializing countries, liberals saw that the new industrial system was causing the rise of new economic power centers, and they gradually become social democrats or democratic socialists precisely so they could protect the democratic method from the undemocratic predations of the new economic elites. (It is one of history's enduring ironies that liberals have to become socialists precisely to save what is most valuable about liberalism.) In the English-speaking countries and in Europe, liberalism survives only as a minority centrist tendency, the territory it once occupied long since taken over by the social democratic, socialist and labor parties - all of which are committed to eventual public ownership of the means of production. America alone is the only industrialized democracy not to have developed a durable democratic Left.

By making a cult out of political liberalism that looked backward to the 19th century for its emotional and cultural cues, Unitarianism played a negative role in American culture, one which partially accounts for its marginalization in American intellectual life. But it also gave it a specific - if increasingly miniscule - role to play in the American cultural establishment, which is always concerned with repressing doubts about the way the economic system is functioning.

Clearly, however, America isn't the only place where institutional evil exists. The disastrous experiments of Stalinist totalitarianism and Mao's Cultural Revolution have killed tens of millions, and still their centralized bureaucracies produce more tyranny and paranoia than quality of life. What we are facing around the world is not just the failure of one or two systems, but a generalized inability to deal with technology and the industrial system itself. Only in a few places, in Scandinavia and western Europe where there are democratic socialist parties, have we begun to see the barest beginnings of that democratic decision-making in the means of production (and the investment process) that can point the way toward a truly human use of the industrial system. And only in the first hesitant steps of the Green parties have we begun to see the emergence of an ecopolitical tradition that can even begin to redress humankind's ravaging of the environment.

So is the answer the wholesale rejection of the industrial system? That is the answer of those waves of bohemia which began with the Romantics and which last surfaced in the Beat and hippie movements of the 1950s and 1960. But it is an unacceptable answer, because it runs away from the problem rather than faces it. We need a political ethic that can seek to humanize industry and technology from within. Above all, we need a political ethic that can denounce and oppose in militant struggle those forces that threaten the human family with nuclear annihilation.

Political liberalism is no longer able to address these questions of good and evil systematically, whether in public life or in the human heart. Nor is it even able to formulate any political strategy against Communism, relying instead on the use of military force, which in the US client states tends simply to become a form of state terrorism. (As George Orwell saw, the only way to beat Stalinism is to offer a Left alternative to it - which means confronting both capitalism *and* Communism.) Since it can neither criticize the systemic nature of greed in American capitalism directly nor offer a Left alternative to Communism, political liberalism is dead.

Religious liberalism is suffering through a parallel crisis. It increasingly understands that orthodox religion is dead,

124

that the old world in which the priest or minister mediated between supernatural agencies and the believer is now gone forever, and that its values must be replaced with a new secular ethic in art, personal morality and in an ethics-based politics. But they do not know what this new secular ethic is to be based upon. I believe that a new secular ethic should be based upon social instincts, as partially understood by 18th-century philosophers, as amended by Mills and the utilitarians, as qualified by Freud and Jung, and as reformulated by recent studies of social evolution and language. This is not the place for a complete explication of my theory, but it is a least a theory, in the sense that I know what I think a new secular ethic ought to be built upon. Most religious liberals do not even go that far. Instead they use vague rhetoric about freedom - but they do not seem to use that freedom to build anything new, nor even anything that is very useful. Embracing freedom means exactly nothing, until and unless one puts that freedom to some kind of test.

Religious liberals also sense that the old dream of millennial justice (the dreams of the Hebrew prophets, and to some extent of Jesus himself) must be replaced by a conscious commitment to social justice. Unless they are willing to go beyond political liberalism, however, they immediately inherit from political liberals all the same liabilities we have just discussed. Religious liberals are particularly noted for their inability to go beyond the taboos of liberal-conservative political debate in America, taboos which are highly charged and which play a specific cultural function, the function of limiting debate.

Such is the power of ideological conditioning, but such also is the special cowardice that seems built into so much of liberal religion. I am not saying that religious liberals should be any more or less cowardly than other Americans; I am simply saying that as long as they accept the taboos of the cultural establishment they will be unable to look at political language and debate with an open mind - and their search for a commitment to social justice that does more than imitate the secular political establishment will be frustrated at the outset.

125

The failure of religious liberals to look at issues of profit and power is disastrous on another count. The real challenge to liberal religion does not come from conservative religion. The real challenge to liberal religion comes from the American worship of power and money. Capitalism and the supposed "laws" of the marketplace are seen as a form of theology, and capital itself is given far-ranging thaumaturgic powers to redeem the Self (a process in which the deliberate sacrifice of the Other is seen as expiatory, and therefore necessary). The market is allowed to function as the older Calvinist God once did, as a brute force that must punish the innocent to prove its power; and in which Success - now defined simply as domination of the Other - takes the place of Salvation. Wealth will not simply be a sign of God's grace, as in the older Calvinist system. Wealth has itself become God.

That is the real religion of modern America, one which has displaced the older established religions, and against which liberal religion is similarly helpless. Liberal religion is helpless because it has failed its own central test, which is that of prophecy. At precisely the time when liberal religion should be warning humanity of the dangers of unrestrained capitalism, of the evil of institutionalized greed, and the nuclear hell with which America's dependence on arms production threatens the world, it is unable to call forth the new political and religious language necessary for such a task. It, too - like the political liberalism it so frequently resembles - is at a dead end.

Because they cannot motivate people to make difficult choices, because they do not understand the systemic nature of evil, because they suffer from institutional cowardice and timidity, both political and religious liberalism have become part of the problem rather than part of the solution. Both forms of liberalism must be transcended. Political liberalism must become some form of democratic socialism; liberal religion must become social religion.

The religious Left offers us a way to go beyond the limits of both political and religious liberalism to a redemption that is both practical and personal liberating.

The pivotal characteristics of social religion begin with

the understanding that a new religious ethic must come from humankind in a natural and historical setting, rather than a supernatural one; that the natural and historical setting of humankind is society; that a commitment to social justice is the key redemptive act; and that this begins with the individual taking responsibility for collective evil. But it also understands that justice is not only a matter of belief, but of emotional orientation and the search for personal fulfillment. It understands, in other words, the emotive roots of the instinct for justice - and the role they can play in everyday life.

Sometimes the process begins with pain - by confronting the victim. When people suffer in your name, there are two things you can do about it. You can make the connection, or you can deny it. If you choose to see what is going on, you must then give it meaning through something you do with your own life. You can do this either through concentrating on the guilt you feel, or by making a commitment that causes you to leave the guilt behind. That is the central challenge of the politics of social justice. That is also the essential religious challenge of our time, because what we are really talking about, in religious terms, is the process of redemption. The two traditions come together at precisely that point where we are willing to confront those issues that most people in America are afraid to talk or think about. That is, in fact, a good modern definition of *prophetic* - the ability to articulate those things that others repress. But prophecy is not a gift from above but a skill that can be learned.

Small groups can teach that skill by validating each group member in her or his struggle toward justice, which is also the struggle to love in an increasingly inhuman world. I am not calling for another top-down committee or project of the kind for which 25 Beacon Street has become famous. I am calling for a grass roots movement of Unitarian Universalists themselves - a revolution from the basement up, as it were, rather than from the top down. I am calling for people to take control of their own religion by inventing new forms for it. I am asking people to take the UU challenge seriously enough to invent new priorities. I am asking people to take freedom seriously enough to actually use that freedom to change their lives. And I am telling you that you can do this without asking permission from 25 Beacon Street.

We know enough about the way the *communidad de base* works in Latin America and the 12-step groups in North America to know that small groups are a powerful new device for human change, that they operate as adoptive families for people searching for ways to articulate and refine their values, and that they also allow people to explore the most intimate kind of emotional orientations. Such groups will also, I think, be the new form of worship for the future, perhaps as part of a new secular religion. But liberation groups in the UU denomination will not happen by themselves. They will have to be formed (invented, if you will) by people who want them and need them.

That brings us to a turning point. This particular pamphlet will have little real value if it does not cause you to seriously consider forming a group. No one will do it for you. You may well fail. But if you fail the first time, you can always try again. And what an adventure that might be! Will you have the courage to form a small group of seven or eight searchers (you can start with two or three) to explore issues of social justice, but also to talk about how issues of power and power-sharing affect you emotionally? It is one thing to know that small groups have a special power. It is another thing to put that special power to work in your life. To do that you must reach out to people and try something you probably have never tried before.

The Unitarian Universalist denomination can build a Left that is completely its own. It can and must be democratic. It can and should minister to emotional as well as political concerns. It can be prophetic, while using the language of secular politics. But at that point that people begin to share their feelings about power, it irrevocably becomes something else - it becomes religious, however secular it may also be. Because at that point when people share their emotions as well as their thoughts, they have become concerned not with seeking power, but with changing the nature of power. And they have begun to do so in their hearts even as they commit themselves to changing it in society.

I began by telling you about Rosario Godoy de Cuevas, and our connection to her. I didn't tell you about her young husband Carlos, who disappeared and was never seen again. (That was why Rosario first became active in the human rights movement in Guatemala - because she could not go on being silent when her husband simply disappeared out of her life one day.) I didn't tell you about Hector Gomez Calito, the leader of the Guatemalan human rights movement who preceded Rosario. (He was tortured to death with a blowtorch, and his tongue was cut out.)

In any case, these are things you may not really want to know very much about. Maybe we hide from these things not because we are evil, but because we are decent. Decent people don't dwell on terrible things, you see. (The German people didn't believe the stories about the camps and the atrocities, either - not because they were evil, but because they were decent.) Decent people don't dwell on evil things.

But religious people do. They are willing to look at evil just long enough to decide what to do about it. If they are conservative evangelicals, they may seek to absolve their guilt through expiatory devices that do not involve making any social commitment. If you believe in social religion, as I do, you will use that pain to make a commitment to social change.

Coffee is the main commercial crop of Guatemala, and also the main export crop. (The economy of Guatemala has been set up to serve the consumer needs of North America, not the needs of Guatemalans.) The Indians who work on the large plantations live in conditions of utter destitution. They are kept that way by the military, which in turn is maintained by the US. (Aided by the Israeli national security establishment, which often arms and trains the most ruthless US client states.) The result is that we can enjoy our coffee for a few pennies less than if the Indians were allowed to live like human beings. Think about that the next time you buy coffee - and the next time you drink it.

But the connection isn't just coffee. It's also in blood. You see, fascism is a system for making money, but it's also a form of totalitarianism. If people like Rosario Godoy de Cuevas were allowed to dissent, peasants' cooperatives and trade unions and political parties of the Left and Center would also have to be allowed - and that would cut down on profit. So people who dissent in any way, people like Rosario, are routinely killed. They die horribly because the rich want you to know they have that kind of power, that they can create that kind of hell on earth.

Think about that, too, the next time you buy or drink coffee.

The powerful people who make American foreign policy are hoping that the few cents you save buying coffee will be enough to keep you silent. It is a kind of bribe. Once you understand that, the meaning of coffee will change - I tell you the taste itself will be different. It will be different because you will have made a connection to the world that demands a choice.

What will you do with that connection? You could hang onto the guilt you feel, if you wish. (That kind of masochistic self-absorption is a major indoor sport among some liberal intellectuals.) Or you can do something better. You can make Rosario's life and death meaningful in your life, on your own terms and in your own way.

You can decide to take that pain and transform it by doing something to transform the system that destroyed her.

The choice is yours.

Like evangelicals, we acknowledge the existence of evil. But we insist on looking at the way it works in the present moment, at the mechanics of evil - and we insist on trying to change that. We are not afraid to look at the faces of those we oppress, nor those who oppress us. When we face that suffering, we have made a choice - and that gives us power. Something else takes the place of pain: the ability to face the demonic and to answer it with love, which is also the power of life over death. That, finally, is the best answer of social religion to the idea of substitutionary atonement. Because we are able in some small way to take personal responsibility for public evil, for us eternity begins now. "Ours the task sublime," go the words of the lovely Universalist hymn, "to build eternity in time."

It is perhaps the greatest paradox of our time that we cannot touch what is timeless and best in ourselves without confronting the demonic nature of collective evil. But what power, what a sense of personal integrity, awaits those of us who are willing to try!

No religion can have meaning in our time without looking at the problem of evil in political terms. The UU Left can be the prophetic minority within our denomination that through art, politics and the search for a new secular ethic can help us make that confrontation. Will there be that prophetic handful with the humor, the sense of adventure, and the unsentimental passion for justice and dialogue to do it? With our denomination's history of social concern and leadership, the UU Left could easily become the natural leader of a larger movement arising from liberal religion generally - and could also supply the political vocabulary and the moral reference points that could allow religious liberalism to transform itself from within.

Lawrence Swaim
Stow, MA
1989

NOTES

1. Gustavo Gutierrez has an excellent discussion on the "Ambiguities in the Term 'Poverty'" in his *A Theology of Liberation*. He focuses on the difference between "material poverty" and "spiritual poverty." (Gutierrez 1973, 288-291).

2. In her essay "Ecofeminism, Reverence For Life, and Feminist Theological Ethics," Lois K. Daly (Birch, Eakin, and McDaniel 1990) provides a well-written synthesis of several liberationist lines of thinking. She spends over half of the essay discussing this key element of Schweitzer's life and thought. She begins by saying:

> Albert Schweitzer's notion of reverence for life provides some clues for feminist theological and ethical efforts to re-examine the relationship between human beings and the nonhuman world and between human beings and God despite the fact that he offers no analysis of oppression. Instead, what Schweitzer does is begin with a description of human beings that link us both with nonhuman nature and with God in a way that does not appear to presuppose those dualistic assumptions of subordination, instrumentality, and polarity. For this reason, his position is highly instructive. *(Daly 96)*

3. There are quite a few sources one could turn to for an appreciation of this relation development, but in few is the relationship between Unitarian Universalism and the American experience directly drawn: instead, the indirect

assumptions are strong (at times overwhelming if not pre-sumptuous). Space won't allow a complete critique of this development, but a shortened summary is possible. Begin-ning with Wilbur (considered a classic among Unitarian Universalists):

> To the Unitarian of today the marks of true religion are spiritual *freedom*, enlightened *reason* and broad and *toler-ant* sympathy, upright character and unselfish worship. These things, which go to the very heart of life, best ex-press the meaning and lesson of Unitarian history. (em-phasis added) *(Wilbur 1925, 470)*

Freedom, reason and tolerance have long been consid-ered the Unitarian Universalist "trinity," essential to the liberal faith tradition. Priestley, Jefferson, the Adams fami-ly, in addition to Stanton, Emerson, Thoreau and Dix are among the many American historical personalities that claimed Unitarian Universalism as their faith and lived out the principles of freedom, reason and tolerance. With bio-graphical sketches of Unitarian Universalist "saints" who lived this "trinity," Fritchman traces this pattern in our na-tional heritage (as well as some European ancestors). (Fritchman 1944)

There are at least two other sources that have been in-strumental in this relation development. A. Powell Davies was one of our Association's greatest leaders, as well as one of the country's most ardent defenders of democracy (Davies 1949). When he spoke about "America's Real Re-ligion," he never spoke about it being Unitarian Universal-ism, but the assumptions were all there. His successor at All Souls in Washington, D.C. followed in his footsteps: Duncan Howlett spoke about "The Fourth American Faith" and like Davies, never named it, but the implications were clear - if only to Unitarian Universalists! (Howlett 1964, xiv)

4. This broad appeal and acceptance on the part of Unitari-an Universalism has the ring of "civil religion" to it. While there are some Unitarian Universalists who like this ap-peal, it is not without its shortcomings. For a good discus-

sion of this, see "Liberation Theology, Civil Religion and the Emerging Church" in King (172).

5. During a discussion of current social issues in a meeting with colleagues, I suggested this point: that our nation was growing so quickly, becoming more diverse and consequently our needs so great that perhaps the old individualism that had seemed to function well for some, might have to be altered. One colleague jumped on this without hesitating: he shared the story of how his grandparents had made a life for themselves under the tenets of individualism, and it's worked for him. He was offended and fed up with those who wanted to "rid" American society of something that had worked so well.

6. The concept and power of objectivation is still a difficult one to discuss. When I delivered a part of this chapter at a study group for colleagues, heads were nodding in understanding and agreement until this sentence. What happened I believe is this: the idea of objective reality is critical to a God concept. Colleagues were ready to agree with the objectivation process with everything but God. In other words, they believed God is the only objective reality! The way I understand this is, too much is at stake in terms of a person's world order to objectivate God. I am not suggesting that God cannot be objective reality, merely that God is personal , objective reality.

7. Spretnak's small book is an excellent primer on Green Politics, and this chapter "Back to Basics" provides a good summary on her "spiritual dimension." She begins the chapter by writing:

> Green politics is about values in our daily lives, how we live and work and play. Core values are informed by deep thinking and existential explorations, which are spiritual perceptions. I would like to consider our core values by exploring three basic questions: Who are we? (or What is our nature?) How shall we relate to our context, the environment? How shall we be related to others? (45)

8. Panentheism is a key concept in Matthew Fox's Creation Spirituality. In his book *Original Blessing*, he defines panentheism:

> ....Now panentheism is not pantheism. Pantheism, which is a declared heresy because it robs God of transcendence, states that "everything is God and God is everything." Panentheism, on the other hand, is altogether orthodox and very fit for orthopraxis as well, for it slips in the little Greek word *en* and thus means, "God is in everything and everything is in God." This experience of the presence of God in our depth and of Dabhar in all the blessings of the sufferings of life is a mystical understanding of God. Panentheism is desperately needed by individuals and religious institutions today. It is the way the creation-centered tradition of spirituality experiences God. (90)

Fox also deals with dualistic themes, for example, original sin/original blessing. The perspective he presents is a unifying, wholistic one that seeks to integrate humankind, God and creation. But perhaps Fox and other creation spirituality followers are attempting too much. McFague writes:

> While the wholistic, planetary perspective leads some to insist that all will be well if a "creation spirituality" were to replace the traditional "redemption spirituality" of the Christian tradition, the issue is not that simple. It is surely the case that the overemphasis on redemption to the neglect of creation needs to be redressed; moreover, there is much in the common creation story that calls us to a profound appreciation of the wonders of our being and the being of all other creatures. Nonetheless, it is doubtful that such knowledge and appreciation will be sufficient to deal with the exigencies of our situation. (*McFague 1991, 15*)

WORKS CITED

Adams, James Luther. 1976. Liberation and epochal thinking. In *On being human religiously: Selected essays in religion and society*, edited by Max L. Stackhouse, 28-32. Boston: Beacon Press

_____. 1976. Guiding principles of a free faith. In *On being human religiously: Selected essays in religion and society*, edited by Max L. Stackhouse, 3-21. Boston: Beacon Press.

_____. 1986. The prophethood of all believers. In *The prophethood of all believers*, edited by George K. Beach, 99-103. Boston: Beacon Press.

_____. 1991. The prophetic covenant and social concern. In *An examined faith: Social Context and religious commitment.* edited by George K. Beach, 234-242. Boston: Beacon Press.

Baum, Gregory. 1989. Community and identity. *In The future of liberation theology: Essays in honor of Gustavo Gutierrez*, ed. Marc H. Ellis and Otto Maduro, 220-228. Maryknoll: Orbis.

Bayer, Charles H. 1986. *A guide to liberation theology for middle class congregations.* St. Louis: CBP Press.

Bellah, Robert N., Richard Madsen, William M. Sullivan, Ann Swidler, and Steven M. Tipton. 1985. *Habits of the heart: Individualism and commitment in American life.* Berkeley: University of California Press.

Berger, Peter L. and Thomas Luckman. 1966. *The social construction of reality: A treatise in the sociology of knowledge.* Garden City: Double Anchor.

Berry, Jason. 1990. A theology for El Salvador. *Washington Post,* 26 November, sec. C, 5.

Berryman, Phillip. 1984. *The religious roots of rebellion.* Maryknoll: Orbis.

_____. 1986. How Christians become socialists. In *Churches in struggle: Liberation theologies and social change in North America,* ed. William K. Tabb, 153-163.

_____. 1987. *Liberation theology: The essential facts about the revolutionary movement in Latin America and beyond.* New York: Pantheon.

Birch, Charles. 1990. Chance, purpose and the order of nature. In *Liberating life: Contemporary approaches to ecological theology,* ed. Charles Birch, William Eakin, and Jay B. McDaniel, 1-5. Maryknoll: Orbis.

Boff, Leonardo. 1989. The originality of the theology of liberation. In *The future of liberation theology: Essays in honor of Gustavo Gutierrez,* ed. Marc H. Ellis and Otto Maduro, 38-48. Maryknoll: Orbis.

Boff, Leonardo and Clodovis. 1987. *Introducing liberation theology.* Maryknoll: Orbis.

Bonino, Jose Miguez. 1983. *Toward a Christian political ethic.* Philadelphia: Fortress.

Brown, Robert McAfree. 1978. *Theology in a new key: responding to liberation themes.* Philadelphia: Westminster Press.

_____. 1988. *Spirituality and liberation: Overcoming the great fallacy.* Philadelphia: Westminister Press.

_____. 1989. Reflections of a North American: The future of liberation theology. In *The future of liberation theology: Essays in honor of Gustavo Gutierrez,* ed. Marc H. Ellis and Otto Maduro, 491-501. Maryknoll: Orbis.

Buechner, Frederick. 1984. *A room called remember: Uncollected pieces.* New York: Harper and Row.

Croatto, J. Severino. 1983. The Gods of oppression. In *The idols of death and the God of life: A theology,* ed. Pablo Richard, 26-45. Maryknoll: Orbis.

Daly, Lois K. 1990. Ecofeminism, reverence for life, and feminist theological ethics. In *Liberating life: Contemporary approaches to ecological theology,* ed. Charles Birch, William Eakin and Jay B. McDaniel, 88-108. Maryknoll: Orbis.

Davies, A. Powell. 1949. *America's real religion.* Boston: Beacon.

de Gruchy, John W. 1986. *Theology and ministry in context: A South African perspective.* Grand Rapids: Eerdmans.

Dorrien, Gary. 1990. Economic democracy. *Christian Century,* 10 September, 274.

Ellis, Marc H. 1987. *Toward a Jewish theology of liberation.* Maryknoll: Orbis.

_____. 1989. Critical thought and messianic trust: Reflections on a Jewish theology of liberation. In *The future of liberation theology: Essay in honor of Gustavo Gutierrez,* ed. Marc H. Ellis and Otto Maduro, 375-389. Maryknoll: Orbis.

Evans, Robert A. and Alice Frazier Evans. 1983. *Human rights: A dialogue between the first and third worlds.* Maryknoll: Orbis.

Fink, Newton. AACTAC: A human process for gathering data and making decisions. A six step process for individuals and groups. Manuscript included in Appendix 2.

Fiorenza, Elisabeth Schussler. 1989 The politics of otherness: Biblical interpretation as a critical praxis for liberation. In *The future of liberation theology: Essays in honor of Gustavo Gutierrez,* ed. Marc H. Ellis and Otto Maduro, 311-325. Maryknoll: Orbis.

Fox, Mathew. 1993. *Original blessing: A primer in creation spirituality.* Santa Fe: Bear & Company.

Fritchman, Stephen Hole. 1944. Men of liberty: *Ten Unitarian pioneers*. Port Washington: Kennikat Press.

Fromm, Erich. 1986. *For the love of life*. New York: The Free Press.

Galilea, Segundo. 1988. *The way of living: A spirituality of liberation*. New York: Harper and Row.

Gilbert, Richard S. 1980. *The prophetic imperative: Unitarian Universalist foundations for a new social gospel*. Boston: UUA.

Goodwin, Ellie. 1992. Nexus of a new environmentalism. *Christianity and Crisis*. 2 March, 54-55.

Granberg-Michaelson, Wesley. 1990. Covenant and Creation. In *Liberating life: Contemporary approaches to ecological theology*. ed. Charles Birch, William Eakin, and Jay B. McDaniel. 27-36. Maryknoll: Orbis.

Gutierrez, Gustavo. 1973. *A theology of liberation: History, politics and salvation*. Maryknoll: Orbis.

_____. 1984. *We drink from our own well: The spiritual journey of a people*. Maryknoll: Orbis.

Hacker, Andrew. 1990. Trans-national America. *The New York Review of Books*, 22 November, 19-24.

Haught, John F. 1990. Religious and cosmic homelessness: Some environmental implications. In *Liberating Life: Contemporary approaches to ecological theology*, ed. Charles Birch, William Eakin, and Jay B. McDaniel. 159-181. Maryknoll: Orbis.

Hedstrom, Ingemar. 1990. Latin America and the need for a life-liberating theology. In *Liberating life: Contemporary approaches to ecological theology*, ed. Charles Birch, William Eakin, and Jay B. McDaniel, 111-124. Maryknoll: Orbis.

Herzog, Frederick. 1988. *God-walk: Liberation shaping dogmatics*. Maryknoll: Orbis.

Hodgson, Peter C. 1988. *Revisioning the church: Ecclesial freedom in the new paradigm*. Philadelphia: Fortress Press.

Howlett, Duncan. 1964. *The fourth American faith*. Boston: Beacon.

Jones, William R. 1973. *Is God a white racist?: A preamble to black theology*. New York: Anchor/Doubleday.

Jones, William R. and Judith Meyer. 1989. *Theology and activism*. Produced by the Unitarian Universalist Association. 45 min. Videocassette.

Keen, Sam. 1988. The stories we live by. *Psychology Today*, December, 44-45.

King, Paul, Ken Maynard, and David O. Woodyard. 1988. *Risking liberation: Middle class powerlessness and social heroism*. Atlanta: John Knox Press.

McDaniel, Jay B. 1990. Revisioning God and the self: Lessons from Buddhism. In *Liberating life: Contemporary approaches to ecological theology*, ed. Charles Birch, William Eakin, and Jay B. McDaniel, 201-227. Maryknoll: Orbis.

McFague, Sallie. 1990. Imaging a theology of nature: The world as God's body. In *Liberating life: Contemporary approaches to ecological theology*. ed. Charles Birch, William Eakin, and Jay B. McDaniel, 201-227. Maryknoll: Orbis.

_____. 1991. An earthly theological agenda. *The Christian Century*, 2-9 January, 12-15.

McGovern, Arthur F. 1989 Dependency theory, Marxist analysis, and liberation theology. In *The future of liberation theology: Essays in honor of Gustavo Gutierrez*, ed., Marc H. Ellis and Otto Maduro, 272-286, Maryknoll: Orbis.

Moyers, Bill. 1989. *God and politics: A kingdom divided*. Produced by Elena Mannes. 90 min. WNET. New York. Videocassette.

Peck, M. Scott. 1987. *The different drum: Community-making and peace.* New York: Simon and Schuster.

Rankin, David. 1978. Thoughts following a suicide. *Portraits from the cross.* Boston: UUA.

Sindima, Harvey. 1990. Community of life: Ecological theology in African perspective. In *Liberating life: Contemporary approaches to ecological theology,* ed. Charles Birch, William Eakin, Jay B. McDaniel, 137-148. Maryknoll: Orbis.

Shaull, Richard. 1984. *Hearlds of a new reformation.* Maryknoll: Orbis.

Sobrino, Jon. 1983. The epiphany of the God of life in Jesus of Nazareth. In *The idols of death and the God of life: A theology.* ed. Pablo Richard, 66-102. Maryknoll: Orbis.

Spretnak, Charlene. 1986. *The spiritual dimension of green politics.* Sante Fe: Bear & Co.

Swaim, Lawrence. 1989. The case for a Unitarian Universalist left. Critique of Unitarian Universalism and the search for liberal religious priorities. Manuscript included in Appendix. 4.

Talvacchia, Kathleen. 1991. Being 'real,' using 'real.' *Christianity and Crisis,* 15 July, 232.

Thandeka. 1989. How black are we? *The World,* January /February, 46.

Unitarian Universalist Association. 1984. Principles and purposes. Boston: UUA.

Vieth, Richard F. 1988. *Holy power, human pain.* Bloomington: Meyer-Stone.

Waldrop, Judith. 1988. A religious accounting. *The World,* July/August, 11-13.

Wilbur, Earl Morse. 1925. *Our Unitarian heritage: An introduction to the history of the Unitarian movement.* Boston: Beacon.

Wright, Conrad. 1989. *Walking together: Polity and participation in Unitarian Universalist churches.* Boston: Skinner House.

Mail Order Information:

For additional copies of *A Reason For Hope*, send $10.00 per book plus $1.50 for shipping and handling (in Maryland add 5% sales tax). Discount for multiple orders. Make checks payable to Fredric J. Muir. Mail c/o Annapolis Unitarian Universalist Church, 333 Dubois Road, Annapolis, MD 21401. Telephone (410) 266-8044.

Also available through local bookstores that use R.R. Bowker Company Books In Print catalogue system. Also order through publisher Sunflower Ink.

144

.